Advanced Plotting

Chris Eboch

Copyright © 2011 Chris Eboch
Pig River Press, Socorro, New Mexico

ISBN-13: 978-1463739300
ISBN-10: 1463739303

Advanced Plotting

by
Chris Eboch

Pig River Press, Socorro, New Mexico

Contents

Why *Advanced Plotting*?

In some ways, plotting a story is simple. A plot involves a character with a problem or goal. The beginning introduces the character's problem or goal, the middle shows that character actively trying to solve the problem or reach the goal, and the end has the character succeeding, or sometimes failing but learning a lesson.

That sounds pretty straightforward. So why is it often so hard to make a plot work well?

I've spoken at local and national writing conferences and given workshops around the world. One of my most popular talks is called "What I Learned from Nancy Drew: Tools for Fast-Paced Plotting." I discovered writers hungry for good advice on plot — not just how to put together a decent plot, but how to take a manuscript and fine-tune that plot into something that works as well as possible.

Advanced Plotting is designed for the intermediate and advanced writer: you've finished a few stories, read books and articles on writing, taken some classes, attended conferences. But you still struggle with plot, or suspect that your plotting needs work.

Maybe you've written short stories but feel intimidated about trying a novel. Maybe you've started novel manuscripts but get stuck partway through, or you've churned out a draft for National Novel Writing Month but don't know how to revise it. Maybe you've finished a manuscript, or even several, but still struggle to interest an editor or agent in your work. Maybe you've published multiple books but wonder if there's a better process for turning a sloppy first draft into a polished final.

This book can help.

Obviously, a manuscript needs more than a strong plot to sell. The best books also have a marketable concept (the "hook"), fascinating characters, an interesting setting, a useful and believable theme, and a strong voice. *Advanced Plotting* doesn't try to teach you everything about writing, but by focusing on plot, you'll have a strong foundation for your work.

In any case, almost everything relates to plot in some way. You'll find advice on using your setting for stronger plotting, using your character's goals and needs to strengthen your plot, and making sure your plot reflects your theme. You'll even find tips on word choice and pacing, which are part of voice. When it comes to writing a great novel, everything ties together — but the foundation is plot.

The Plot Outline Exercise is designed to help a writer work with a completed manuscript to identify and fix plot weaknesses. It can also be used to help flesh out an outline. Additional articles address specific plot challenges, such as getting off to a fast start, propping up a sagging middle, building to a climax, and improving your pacing. Guest authors share advice from their own years of experience.

Read the book straight through, study the index to find help with your current problem, or dip in and out randomly — however you use this book, you'll find fascinating insights and detailed tips to help you build a stronger plot and become a better writer.

About the Author

Advanced Plotting is my 14th book in print. As Chris Eboch, I write for children. My novels for ages nine and up include *The Eyes of Pharaoh*, a mystery set in ancient Egypt; *The Well of Sacrifice*, a Mayan adventure; and the Haunted series: *The Ghost on the Stairs, The Riverboat Phantom, The Knight in the Shadows*, and *The Ghost Miner's Treasure*. (You can read samples at www.chriseboch.com.)

I also write for adults as Kris Bock. *Rattled* launches my romantic suspense series featuring treasure hunting adventures in the Southwest. (You can read the first three chapters at www.krisbock.com.)

Besides those published books, I've finished eight other novel manuscripts. A couple were the victims of market forces, but many were simply unsuccessful. My files also show a number of false starts, where I got stuck a few chapters in, plus dozens of unpublished short stories and articles. All these were learning experiences.

I learn even more by teaching others. I've critiqued over a hundred novels and a thousand short stories. If that doesn't teach you what works and what doesn't, nothing will!

I love the creative side of writing, but I'm also analytical — I love to break down writing to see how and why it works. And I like to share what I learn in workshops and articles. *Advanced Plotting* includes adaptations of my writing articles previously printed in *Writer's Digest, Children's Writer*, or one of the annual *Writer's Guides* from Writer's Institute Publications.

I use my novels as examples in this book. I'm not claiming my work is the best out there, but I *know* my own work best and can explain the challenges I faced and solutions I found. (Plus, I don't have to worry about getting permission to quote someone else.) I've also invited other authors to share their insights, to give a broader view of how authors approach plot.

What Is the Plot Outline Exercise?

It's hard for writers to judge their own work. Sometimes we are so in love with the ideas and characters that we can't see the flaws in the manuscript. Sometimes we know what we wanted to convey, so we don't realize we didn't put it clearly on the page. Sometimes we're just not experienced enough to recognize the problems, let alone know how to fix them.

Critique groups can help, and I recommend them wholeheartedly. A good critique group is worth its weight in chocolate. But critique groups can suffer from some of the same problems as the individual writer. Some critiquers are great as cheerleaders, line editors, or grammar mavens, but don't know how to see the big picture. Some may sense problems but not know how to offer advice for fixing them. Some may not be confident enough to speak up or may hesitate to offer tough advice for fear of offending or interfering with the author's vision.

In addition, many critique groups look at a manuscript a few pages at a time, so it takes months or years to critique a novel. By the end of the experience, who can really remember how well the beginning tied in with the end, whether the characters remained consistent, and whether all the subplots got resolved? Plus, if the author has been answering questions or explaining the piece along the way, the critique group members have inside information a new reader will not.

The Plot Outline Exercise can be used with a critique group and would be great for a writing retreat. It can also be used when you're on your own. The goal is to first help you step back from the manuscript and view it as a whole, so you can see the big picture. This will help you find places where something is missing, redundant, or otherwise unnecessary; sections that don't make sense or don't fit smoothly into the whole; and other problems. Once you understand the big picture problems, you can start seeing how to fix them. From there you can narrow your focus to the chapter, scene, and paragraph level, finding and fixing smaller flaws. Using the Plot Outline Exercise is like having an experienced teacher analyze your work and point out the trouble spots.

If you are an outliner, you can also use the Plot Outline Exercise to analyze your outline before you start writing. This can save a lot of time in the long run. I explain the process in The Plot Exercise for Outlining.

I designed the Plot Outline Exercise for use with novels, but you can also use it for short stories, picture books, narrative nonfiction, memoirs, and other formats. Skip the questions that aren't relevant — but consider them seriously first, to see if they might have some useful insight.

One warning — like exercises for your body, these exercises won't help if you don't actually do them. You can vary the details to better suit your needs, but if you make a halfhearted effort, you'll get halfhearted results.

Take the time to do the Plot Outline Exercise properly. You may be overwhelmed when you start to realize how much work you have left to do. Put down your manuscript for a while and do something fun. Then come back ready to work. Think of all the energy you put into the first draft. You don't want to waste all that time and effort! If you start submitting or self-publishing your story before it's ready, or if you just give up, you are throwing away those hours of hard work. Make them count, and make your manuscript shine, by devoting the necessary time to revisions.

The Plot Outline Exercise

Follow these steps to make an outline of your manuscript. Focus first on making notes; save the actual editing until after you have detailed notes about what changes you need to make.

Write a one or two sentence synopsis for your manuscript.

What genre is it? What is it (briefly) about? This might be the equivalent of your thirty-second pitch with your "hook," but don't worry about making it pretty. The goal is to give yourself something you can refer back to as a reminder of what the manuscript is really about. Here are a couple of examples:

Rattled is a romantic suspense novel set in the dangerous New Mexico desert. Erin, her best friend Camie, and love interest Drew head to the desert to search for a lost treasure, but they face dangers from nature, wild animals, and criminals out to steal the treasure.

The Eyes of Pharaoh is a mystery set in ancient Egypt, for ages nine and up. When their best friend disappears, Seshta and Horus spy on merchants, soldiers, and royalty, and fall into a dangerous trap as they uncover a plot against Egypt.

The Well of Sacrifice is a middle grade adventure set in the waning days of the Mayan civilization. A Mayan girl battles the evil high priest who is trying to take over the city.

In these examples, the first sentences identify the genre, setting, and age range. You probably have those things firmly in your mind, but it doesn't hurt to have this reminder, especially those keywords *suspense, mystery,* and *adventure.* That reminds me that I shouldn't spend too much time exploring the history and culture of ancient Egypt, for example; the mystery should come first.

The second sentences in each synopsis summarize the plot in a few words. This is tricky when you have several important characters and two or three hundred pages of plot twists. But before you do anything else, spend some time trying to identify the plot at its most basic, core level. Usually that comes down to identifying the main character (MC) and what he or she is trying to achieve.

Depending on the type of novel, your primary focus may be on the internal or on the external journey.

I could have written the second sentence for *The Eyes of Pharaoh* like this instead: When Seshta's best friend disappears, she has to choose between finding him and preparing for the contest that could launch her career as a dancer.

That would focus more on the main character's internal conflict, instead of her external challenges. That is also an important part of the novel, and if I felt it was important enough, perhaps I'd add another sentence to the synopsis. But once again, this is a mystery, and above all else I wanted to make sure I had an action-packed plot. Seshta's emotional journey adds depth to the novel, but it's not what I want readers to notice most.

If you're having trouble identifying your plot in a sentence or two, think about how your ideal reader might briefly describe the plot in casual conversation. For example, I might imagine a 10-year-old saying about *The Eyes of Pharaoh*, "It's this great mystery story where they have to follow these clues and investigate people." He's not going to focus on the main character's personal choices or emotional journey.

You can be a little flexible with your synopsis length, if you really need to, but this isn't an exercise in packing the maximum amount of information into a rambling, run-on sentence. Rather, this is an attempt to distill your idea down into its most basic form. You're not trying to impress an agent or editor; this is just for your own use. It doesn't have to be pretty, but it should be simple.

Define your goal.

Do you want an action-packed page turner? A novel that explores an issue and makes people think? A laugh-out-loud funny book for reluctant reader boys? A literary masterpiece in the style of books that win major awards? There is no right or wrong answer, just your personal goal for this manuscript. As with the synopsis, the goal is to give you a simple reminder you can refer to when you're making decisions about what to add, cut, or change in the manuscript.

Outline.

If you hate outlining, don't be intimidated by the word. If you do outline, you can do this exercise with your outline, before you write your first draft. However, it's fine to write a draft of the novel first and then worry about outlining. You can even write two or three or ten drafts before you try this exercise. You don't need Roman numerals or subheads, just a brief description of what happens. The outline is simply a record of what you have written.

Think of it as the equivalent of a photo album of your vacation. If you try to remember what happened on your vacation, you might get confused about what you did on each day, and you might even forget some of the highlights. A chronological photo album, with just one photo per event, helps you keep your thoughts organized while triggering memories of each event. Writing an outline after you finish a draft of your novel helps you see what you have so you can step back and look at the big picture.

For every chapter, write a sentence describing what happens. If you have long chapters with multiple scenes, you may want to do this for each scene rather than each chapter. If you are doing this exercise on paper rather than the computer, leave plenty of space after each chapter summary for your notes — at least three or four blank lines. This is where you will be making notes about what changes you need to make in the manuscript. While you are making your chapter/scene notes, you should also:

Make a note of the number of pages in each chapter.

For each scene/chapter, list the emotions you've portrayed. Underline or highlight the major emotion.

Keep track of subplots by briefly mentioning what happens in each chapter where that subplot appears. Use a different color of pen or highlighter for each subplot. For example, you might use a purple pen to keep track of the romantic subplot and a green pen to track a subplot with the main character's father.

Analyze Your Plot

Now that you have an outline of your manuscript, including the main action, subplots and emotions, you're ready to analyze your plot. You're not going to start editing yet, just analyzing and making notes. This exercise will guide you through that.

The Plot Outline Exercise is designed to start big and then focus in on details. If you look over all the questions in advance, you might start to feel overwhelmed. The key is to take things one step at a time. Consider each question individually and spend time on it. If you read a question and immediately think, "Oh, that part is fine. I'm happy with that," slow down. Take another look at your synopsis and goal, and then look through your outline carefully with that question in mind. Have you really done all you can, or are you just in a hurry?

In a similar vein, you may be tempted to dismiss certain questions because you feel they don't apply to your manuscript. That's fine — it's your story and you ultimately make all decisions. If you have a good reason for doing something unusual, such as starting with the focus on someone other than the main character, go for it. Rules can be broken, if handled well. But before you immediately dismiss the question, consider it seriously. Be sure that you really made an intelligent decision based on your specific goals, and aren't just trying to skip a question because you don't want to go through the work of major revisions. Our minds can be sneaky about trying to convince us to take the easy way out.

Don't plan to do the entire analysis in one day. Instead, you might look only at the Conflict questions on one day, tackle the Tension questions the next day, and spend separate days on Subplots and Secondary Characters and Theme. Or you might even need several days to get through one section.

Don't make revisions on your manuscript as you answer these questions. Instead, identify trouble spots and use your outline to make notes about the changes you need to make in each scene or chapter. Otherwise, you may spend days making major changes to increase your conflict, and then based on a later question decide to cut a character or subplot. You'll save time by planning your changes in advance before you start your revisions.

The Fine Tuning section is a bit different. That's where you look at everything from logic to language use. You may want to make your major revisions before you dive into Fine Tuning, though I recommend that you at least glance over those questions before you revise. One or two of them may trigger the realization that you need to make a major change in something like your point of view.

When you do get to the Fine Tuning section, don't rush through that either — you might need to spend an entire revision session on one question in order to get the most out of it. The results will be worth it.

If you are having trouble visualizing how this is supposed to look, you'll find an example at the end of this section, after the list of questions.

Analyze Your Plot Outline for Conflict:

- Put a check mark by the line if there is conflict in that chapter. For chapters where there is no conflict: can you cut them, interweave them with other chapters, or add new conflict? The conflict can be physical danger, emotional stress, or both, so long as the main character (MC) is facing a challenge. — *See the article on Characters in Conflict, p. 39*

- Where do we learn what the main conflict is? Could it be sooner? Is there some form of conflict at the beginning, even if it is not the main conflict? Does it at least relate to the main conflict? The inciting incident — the problem that gets the story going — should happen as soon as possible, but not until the moment is ripe. The reader must have enough understanding of the character and situation to make the incident meaningful. Too soon, and the reader is confused. Too late, and the reader gets bored first. — *See the articles on Plotting Like a Screenwriter, p. 43, The Hollywood Touch, p. 60, and The Promise of the First Chapter, p. 66*

- Where do we learn the stakes? What are they? Do you have positive stakes (what the MC will get if he succeeds), negative stakes (what the MC will suffer if he fails), or best of all, both? Could the penalty for failure be worse? Your MC should not be able to walk away without penalty. — *See the articles on Developing Your Idea into a Story, p. 26, Tips on Plotting Your Novel, p. 30, and Characters in Conflict, p. 39*

- What is the MC's flaw? Do you use this throughout the story to add complications and make challenges more difficult? Should the character make a bad decision or lose hope at one or more points? — *See the articles on Developing Your Idea into a Story, p. 26, Tips on Plotting Your Novel, p. 30, Characters in Conflict, p. 39, and Plot Turning Points, p. 52*

- Is the main conflict resolved at the climax, and is the climax at the end of the book? — *See the articles on Developing Your Idea into a Story, p. 26, Plotting Like a Screenwriter, p. 43, and Plot Turning Points, p. 52*

- Do you end fairly quickly after the climax, while wrapping up any loose ends and leaving the reader satisfied? You don't need to end immediately after the climax, as many readers like to bask in a happy ending, but don't ramble on for dozens of pages after the dramatic ending, and don't end in the middle of nothing happening. You should end with something dramatic, meaningful, and appropriate to the story, whether exciting, funny, touching, or sad. — *See the article on Plotting Like a Screenwriter, p. 43*

- What's the timeframe? Can you tighten it? Can you add a "ticking clock," where the MC has limited time to succeed?

- Does anything need to be cut, added, or moved? If you have a minimum or maximum length, work on that here. — *See the articles on Add More Meat to Your Manuscript, p. 55, and The Hollywood Touch, p. 60*

Analyze Your Plot Outline for Tension:

- Does each scene fulfill the synopsis goal? Does it advance plot, reveal character, or ideally both? — *See the articles on The Hollywood Touch, p. 60, and How to Write Vivid Scenes, p. 74*

- Does each scene have a goal, such as a shorter term goal that helps lead to the final goal? Can you make the stakes higher for any scenes? — *See the article on How to Write Vivid Scenes, p. 74*

- Mark plot twists. Do you have several surprises/reversals? If not, can you add some? — *See the articles on Plot: Not Just Another Word for a Hole in a Graveyard, p. 34, Plotting Like a Screenwriter, p. 43, Plot Turning Points, p. 52, and Add More Meat to Your Manuscript, p. 55*

- Is the antagonist actively thwarting the hero throughout the book? If you don't have a human antagonist, could you make the book stronger by adding one or more, even if they're minor characters? Or could one of the other secondary characters take on an antagonistic role — perhaps a parent interfering with a child's plan, or a difficult classmate, teacher, coworker, or boss? Even a friend can cause trouble, if that friend has different needs or goals from your MC. — *See the articles on Characters in Conflict, p. 39, Add More Meat to Your Manuscript, p. 55, and On the Edge of Your Seat: Creating Suspense, p. 63*

- Does your MC attempt to make progress toward his/her primary goal in every chapter, or are some chapters only subplot? If you have chapters that are purely subplot, can you weave them into other chapters with plot, or add plot progression within those chapters?

- Does the tension vary but ultimately rise over time, with the situation worsening? Can you increase the complications so that at each step more is at stake and there's greater risk or a better reward? If the tension stays the same, the story will feel flat, even if the tension stays high. This is a common cause of sagging middles. You want ups and downs with an overall sense of increasing trouble. — *See the articles on Developing Your Idea into a Story, p. 26, Plotting Like a Screenwriter, p. 43, and Add More Meat to Your Manuscript, p. 55*

- How many emotions do you have in each chapter/scene? Can you add ups and downs? You want strong emotion, but you also want variety. For example, your MC could feel happy anticipation, then anxiety that things aren't going as planned, followed by a shock, which causes humiliation, then anger, then despair. That's much more dramatic than just having a character angry for a whole scene. — *See the article on Characters in Conflict, p. 39*

- Do the MC's emotions escalate over time? As the tension rises, the emotions should get stronger as well. — *See the article on The Unity of Character and Plot, p. 93*

- Are the most important and dramatic events written out in moment-by-moment detail, so we feel like we are in the scene? Save summary for less dramatic sections where you want to convey information quickly. — *See the article on How to Write Vivid Scenes, p. 74*

Analyze Your Main Character:

- Do you have a single main character? Can the reader identify the MC at the start of the story? Does the story maintain its focus on that character throughout? If you have several MCs, is that the best choice for this story?

- Is your MC well developed, so he or she feels like a real person? Does she have strengths and weaknesses that play into the plot? Does she have quirks that make her interesting and well-rounded? Is her personality and behavior consistent throughout the manuscript? Will your readers like and identify with the character to some extent? — *See the articles on Developing Your Idea into a Story, p. 26, Tips on Plotting Your Novel, p. 30, Characters in Conflict, p. 39, and The Unity of Character and Plot, p. 93*

- If you have several MCs, are they all equally well developed? Do they each have a consistent, major role in the manuscript?

- Does your MC control the story, staying active and making decisions? Does he solve the problem at the end? Avoid having an MC who is simply a victim throughout the story or who is rescued by outside forces at the climax. — *See the articles on Developing Your Idea into a Story, p. 26, Characters in Conflict, p. 39, and Plot Turning Points, p. 52*

- Are you in your MC's point of view (POV)? If not, is that the best decision? Would you be better off switching viewpoint so the reader feels closer to or farther from the character? If you have several viewpoint characters, is each viewpoint strong, consistent, and appropriate? If you are trying to use omniscient viewpoint, are you truly omniscient, or are you really awkwardly jumping between viewpoints? — *See the article On the Edge of Your Seat: Creating Suspense, p. 63*

Analyze Your Subplots and Secondary Characters:

- Look at your subplots. Are they woven evenly throughout the manuscript? Do you need to give more attention to some or space them out more evenly? — *See the article on Add More Meat to Your Manuscript, p. 55*
- If you have a lot of secondary characters, can any be combined or eliminated? Do you have more than one secondary character filling the same job? For example, if the MC has two best friends who are essentially the same and are both supportive, either eliminate one or change her so she has a different role. — *See the articles on Developing Your Idea into a Story, p. 26, and Add More Meat to Your Manuscript, p. 55*

Analyze Your Plot Outline for Theme:

- Do you touch on your theme throughout the manuscript? Are there places where you can add references, perhaps oblique, to set it up better? — *See the articles on Developing Your Idea into a Story, p. 26, and Message, Moral, Meaning: The Theme, p. 85*
- Look at your character arc. Does the MC experience an epiphany? Does she see herself differently at the end? How will she behave differently now? (This might not apply to novels that are part of long series, such as mysteries, where the MC can't change too much in a single book. Still, a minor epiphany, insight, or change of view can add emotional impact to your ending.)

Fine Tuning:

For this section, you need to look at the manuscript itself, rather than just the outline. You may want to make your major revisions to characters, plot, and content before you tackle these details. Depending on how much revision you had to do based on your notes from the previous sections of the Plot Outline Exercise, you may even want to make another outline and answer the earlier questions again, before you start polishing. Deal with the big picture items first before you start fine-tuning.

- Do you have a strong, dramatic opening? — *See the articles on The Hollywood Touch, p. 60, The Promise of the First Chapter, p. 66, and Hook 'Em Fast, p. 71*
- Look at cause and effect. Does each scene lead logically to the next? Are they in the proper order? Are any redundant? If you cut the scene, would you lose anything? — *See the article on How to Write Vivid Scenes, p. 74*
- Do you have transitions between scenes, so the reader always knows how much time has passed, where the characters are, who's on stage, and who the POV character is (if you have multiple POVs)?
- Is your POV consistent?
- Do you include all the clues your readers need for the story to make sense and feel believable? — *See the article On the Edge of Your Seat: Creating Suspense, p. 63*
- How long are your chapters? Do you have any unusually long or short ones? Should you make changes?
- Where are your cliffhanger moments? Do they match chapter breaks? If not, should they? Can you add more cliffhangers? For most types of novels, you don't want too many chapters to end happily. Even if the character has just had a success, keep tension high by having him looking toward the next challenge. — *See the articles on Add More Meat to Your Manuscript, p. 55, and Hanging by the Fingernails: Cliffhangers, p. 80*
- Can you expand your strongest scenes for more drama? — *See the articles on The Hollywood Touch, p. 60, How to Write Vivid Scenes, p. 74, and Hanging by the Fingernails: Cliffhangers, p. 80*
- Check for accuracy. Are your facts correct? Are your characters and setting consistent? If you include details of seasons, days of the week, or times of day, you may want to make a calendar to ensure that you don't have a full moon on one night and a crescent moon the next, or a week's worth of activity between Monday and Wednesday
- Do you use your setting to add color and drama? — *See the articles on Tips on Plotting Your Novel, p. 30, and Add More Meat to Your Manuscript, p. 55*
- Do you have dynamic language: Strong, active verbs? A variety of sentence and paragraph lengths? No clichés?
- Do you show rather than tell? Do you avoid words that explain emotion (*angry, joyfully, with annoyance*) and instead let the reader see the character's emotion through their actions, gestures, dialog, and thoughts? — *See the articles On the Edge of Your Seat: Creating Suspense, p. 63, and How to Write Vivid Scenes, p. 74*

- Do you bring your scenes to life with multiple senses (sight, sound, taste, smell, touch)?
- Look just at your dialog. Does each major character have a unique voice that is consistent throughout the manuscript? (Try reading just that character's dialog aloud.) Is the dialog lively and interesting, often advancing the plot and increasing tension? Is it believable — but not realistic, since real conversations are often too rambling and dull when put on the page? Can you trim the dialog to improve the pace, cutting out the boring "How are you?" parts and getting to the good stuff? — *See the article on Five Revision Passes (ok, seven maybe. . .), p. 89*
- Do you have a balance of action and dialogue, with just enough vivid description to set the scene? — *See the articles on The Hollywood Touch, p. 60, and Five Revision Passes (ok, seven maybe. . .), p. 89*
- Do you vary your paragraph and sentence lengths, using shorter paragraphs and sentences to bring out the drama of action scenes? — *See the article on Hanging by the Fingernails: Cliffhangers, p. 80*
- Finally, edit for spelling and punctuation.

As you use the Plot Outline Exercise, you may come up with additional questions. Make notes on anything you want to cover when you use the exercise with future manuscripts. You can download a copy of the Plot Outline Exercise from my Kris Bock website (www.krisbock.com) to more easily edit it to suit your own needs.

An Example of the Exercise

As an example of how the Plot Outline Exercise might look, here is an outline of the opening scenes of my unpublished middle grade novel, *The Mountain*, featuring a 12-year-old boy who runs into mysterious people while hiking in the woods. For the purpose of this book, I've used italics instead of colored pen for the subplot.

Chapter 1, 12 pages: Jesse plans fishing trip while dealing with family secrets. Conflict — yes. Emotions — Jesse is angry and resentful. *Subplot — family secrets.*

Notes: Delete opening scene and start the next day when Jesse is ready to leave. Bring his father into the scene, showing the distance between them. Trim chapter to get Jesse out of the house and into the woods quickly — move scene with Becca to later in the book.

Chapter 2, seven pages: Jesse goes hiking, follows tracks, and meets a woman in the woods. Conflict — tension, but no major conflict. Emotions — confidence, then curiosity.

Notes: Cut scenery to get to action sooner. Have Jesse briefly get annoyed at *family secrets* while hiking. Increase conflict by having him notice blood on the trail.

Chapter 3, scene one, six pages: Jesse helps Maria. Conflict — tension, but no major conflict. Emotions — Jesse gets schoolboy crush on the older Maria.

Notes: Include Maria's brother Rick in the scene and have them acting nervous to increase sense of mystery. Include a cliffhanger moment with Maria asking Jesse to promise not to tell anyone he's seen them, and end chapter.

Chapter 3, scene two, five pages: Jesse fishes and then goes back to Maria. Conflict — none. Emotions — proud of his abilities.

Notes: Include more varied emotions. Have him remember fishing with dad and ponder the *family secrets*. Have him wonder more about these strangers. Include first scene from next chapter when Shaw shows up, to end on a dramatic moment.

Outlining the book this way showed me several important things about the opening chapters. First of all, after some conflict in the first chapter, I had two chapters, one of them very long, with no major conflict. Since this is a suspense novel, I needed to increase the conflict. I also needed to pick up the pace, deleting some of the description. I had a good scene with his little sister Becca in the first chapter, but it didn't need to be there. I could get Jesse into the woods more quickly by moving that scene to the next time he is at home. And I needed the strangers in the woods to be more mysterious early on.

I also noticed that I dropped the family secrets subplot through much of the book, because Jesse is not at home most of the time. I needed to find ways to include that, if only by having him think about it.

Your format may be different — for example, you may want to make columns for Chapter Number, Number of Pages, Conflict, and Emotions, so you don't have to keep writing the words. You may choose to do this as a computer document, a spreadsheet, or with handwritten notes on paper (just remember to leave plenty of room for notes after each chapter.) You may have more notes on each chapter and you may find a different way to organize them. Do what works for you.

Using The Plot Exercise when Outlining

Not everyone can write a detailed outline before they start writing a manuscript. Not everyone wants to. (See Plotting by the Seat of Your Pants, by Susanne Alleyn, on page 36 in this book.)

I used an outline for my first novel, *The Well of Sacrifice*, but I didn't wind up following it at all. I was inspired to write the book by the idea of a Mayan girl being thrown into a sacrificial *cenote* and surviving. I thought I would start the book with that scene. But then I decided the reader would need some background — they needed to know about her brother, and about the savages who were making raids on the city, and about why the city was in such trouble.... The scene with the sacrificial well wound up in Chapter 20.

As I learned more about writing and developed my skills, I started to use outlines more effectively. When an editor from *Aladdin* was interested in my *Haunted* series about kids who travel with a ghost hunter TV show, he wanted to see outlines for the second and third book along with the completed first manuscript. Those outlines weren't too hard, because I already had a well-developed concept and characters, and I could use the first manuscript to judge how many chapters, scenes, and plot twists I needed.

When I decided to write my first novel for adults, I started with an outline because I wanted to make sure I had enough material to fill 85,000 words, instead of the 35,000 I was used to for children's novels. I developed a detailed, 15-page outline that acted as a guide when writing the book. Because the outline covered everything from the major action to the character arcs and subplots, I turned out a draft so solid that my critique group members said it felt like a book "off the shelf." (Actually, I count the outline as the first draft, and I edited each chapter before sending it to the group, so they really saw the third draft. But regardless, I saved myself an enormous amount of time by doing much of the plot editing before I ever started writing the manuscript.) As you can see, I have become a believer in outlines.

If you prefer to start with an outline, or if you think you might like to try that for a change, you can use the Plot Outline Exercise before you start writing your first draft. You won't be able to address every question, but you'll have the answers to many of them in your outline.

You can look at each scene for conflict, adjusting those that don't have enough. You can study your character arcs and decide if you want your characters to change more. You can check your subplots to ensure that they are properly balanced throughout the manuscript. Use your colored highlighter for this. In one outline, I highlighted a couple of important secondary characters, including the MC's sister. I realized that she appeared at the beginning and the end, but not much in the middle, so I figured out ways to include her in some of those middle scenes.

Whether you're an outliner or a "seat-of-the-pants" writer, I hope you'll find the Plot Outline Exercise helpful at some stage of your writing.

Essays on the Craft of Writing

The Plot Outline Exercise is the core of this book. However, in reality, identifying the flaws in your manuscript is just the first step. You have to be able to fix them, and that introduces a new host of challenges. The following essays address common trouble spots. Many of these essays are adapted from my previously published articles or from notes from workshops I've taught.

I also invited other published authors to share their thoughts on plotting challenges. Many of their essays were first published as blog posts. I hope that including other voices in this literary conversation will show how different writers develop their own techniques for strong plotting, while emphasizing some of the common threads.

Browse through the articles or focus on the one that addresses your current problem. Either way, you'll find lots of great advice.

Developing Your Idea into a Story

by Chris Eboch

People often ask writers, "Where do you find your ideas?" But for a writer, the more important question is, "What do I do with my idea?"

If you have a "great idea," but can't seem to go anywhere with it, you probably have a premise rather than a complete story plan. A story has four main parts: situation, complications, climax, and resolution. You need all of them to make your story work.

The situation should involve an interesting main character with a challenging problem or goal. Even this takes development. Maybe you have a great challenge, but aren't sure why a character would have that goal. Or maybe your situation is interesting, but doesn't actually involve a problem.

For example, I wanted to write about a brother and sister who travel with a ghost hunter TV show. The girl can see ghosts, but the boy can't. That gave me the characters and situation, but no problem or goal. Goals come from need or desire. What did they want that could sustain a series?

Tania feels sorry for the ghosts and wants to help them, while keeping her gift a secret from everyone but her brother. Jon wants to help and protect his sister, but sometimes feels overwhelmed by the responsibility. Now we have characters with problems and goals. The story is off to a strong start.

Tips:

- Make sure your idea is specific and narrow. Focus on an individual person and situation, not a universal concept. For example, don't try to write about "racism." Instead, write about one character facing racism in a particular situation.

- Ask why the goal is important to the character. The longer the story, the higher the stakes needed to sustain it. A short story character might want to win a contest; a novel character might need to save the world.

- Ask why this goal is difficult. The level of difficulty will vary depending on the length of the story and the age of the character, but the task should be believably hard.

- Even if your main problem is external, give the character an internal flaw that contributes to the difficulty. This adds complications and also makes your character seem more real. For some internal flaws, see the seven deadly sins: lust, gluttony, greed, sloth, wrath, envy, and pride.
- Test the idea. Change the character's age, gender, or looks. Change the POV, setting, external conflict, internal conflict. Choose the combination that has the most dramatic potential.

Building the Middle

If a character solves his goal easily, the story is boring. To keep tension high, you need complications.

For short stories, try the "rule of three" and have the main character try to solve the problem three times. The first two times, he fails and the situation worsens. Remember: the situation should worsen. If things stay the same, he still has a problem, but the tension is flat. If his first attempts make things worse, tension rises.

For novels, you may have even more attempts and failures. In my first Haunted book, *The Ghost on the Stairs*, I made sure each ghost encounter felt more dangerous. As Tania tries to get closer to the ghost in order to help her, Jon worries that she will go too far and be injured or even killed. With enough variety, you can sustain this kind of tension indefinitely (witness the ongoing battle between Harry and Voldemort in the seven-book Harry Potter series).

You can worsen the situation in several ways. The main character's actions could make the challenge more difficult. In my children's mystery set in ancient Egypt, *The Eyes of Pharaoh*, a young temple dancer searches for her missing friend. But when she asks questions at the barracks where he was a soldier, she attracts dangerous attention from his enemies.

The villain may also raise the stakes. In my Mayan historical drama, *The Well of Sacrifice*, the main character escapes a power-hungry high priest. He threatens to kill her entire family, forcing her to return to captivity.

Secondary characters can cause complications, too, even if they are not "bad guys." In *The Ghost on the Stairs*, the kids' mother decides to spend the day with them, forcing them to come up with creative ways to investigate the ghost while under her watchful eyes.

Finally, the main character may simply run out of time. At her first attempt, she had a week. At her second attempt, she had a day. Those two attempts have failed, and now she has only an hour! That creates tension.

- Tip: For each turning point in the story, brainstorm 10 things that could happen next. Then pick the one that is the worst or most unexpected, so long as it is still believable for the story.

Can She Do It?!

Your character has faced complications through the middle of the story. Finally, at the climax, the main character must succeed or fail. Time is running out. The race is near the end. The girl is about to date another guy. The villain is starting the battle. One way or another, your complications have set up a situation where it's now or never. However you get there, the climax will be strongest if it is truly the last chance. You lose tension if the reader believes the main character could fail this time, and simply try again tomorrow.

In my new romantic suspense novel, *Rattled*, the climax comes when the heroine is chained to the floor of a cave by a villain threatening to kill her and her friends. If she can escape, maybe she can stop the bad guys and save her friends. But the penalty for failure is death — the highest stake of all. Short stories, different genres, or novels for younger kids might have lesser stakes, but the situation should still be serious.

Tips:

- Don't rush the climax. Take the time to write the scene out in vivid detail, even if the action is happening fast. Think of how movies switch to slow motion, or use multiple shots of the same explosion, in order to give maximum impact to the climax. Use multiple senses and your main character's thoughts and feelings to pull every bit of emotion out of the scene.

- To make the climax feel fast-paced, use mainly short sentences and short paragraphs. The reader's eyes move more quickly down the page, giving a sense of breathless speed. (This is a useful technique for cliffhanger chapter endings as well.)

Happy Endings

The climax ends with the resolution. You could say that the resolution finishes the climax, but it comes from the situation: it's how the main character finally meets that original challenge.

In almost all cases the main character should resolve the situation himself. No cavalry to the rescue! Today, even romance novels rarely have the hero saving the heroine; she at least helps out. We've been rooting for the main character to succeed, so if someone else steals the climax away from him or her, it robs the story of tension and feels unfair.

Here's where many beginning children's writers fail. It's tempting to have an adult — a parent, grandparent, or teacher, or even a fairy, ghost, or other supernatural creature — step in to save the child or tell him what to do. But kids are inspired by reading about other children who tackle and resolve problems. It helps them believe that they can meet their challenges, too. When adults take over, it shows kids as powerless and dependent on grownups. So regardless of your character's age, let your main character control the story all the way to the end (though others may assist).

Although your main character should be responsible for the resolution, she doesn't necessarily have to succeed. She might, instead, realize that her goals have changed. The happy ending then comes from her new understanding of her real needs and wants. Some stories may even have an unhappy ending, where the main character's failure acts as a warning to readers. This is more common in literary novels than in genre fiction.

Tips:

How the main character resolves the situation — whether she succeeds or fails, and what rewards or punishments she receives — will determine the theme. To help focus your theme, ask yourself:

- What am I trying to accomplish?
- Who am I trying to reach?
- Why am I writing this?

Once you know your theme, you know where the story is going and how it must be resolved. For example, a story with the theme "Love conquers all" would have a different resolution than a story with the theme "Love cannot always survive great hardship."

The next time you have a great idea but can't figure out what to do with it, see if you have all four parts of the story. If not, see if you can develop that idea into a complete, dramatic story or novel by expanding your idea, complications, climax or resolution, as needed. Then readers will be asking you, "Where did you get that fabulous idea?"

Tips on Plotting Your Novel

by Janice Hardy

Story ideas can come from anywhere, and those are the easy part of writing. It's figuring out what to do *past* that glimmer of an idea where it can get tricky. How do you get your protagonist from that opening scene to the end? How do you know what problems to throw in their way? Let's look at some common places ideas start and look for ways to find a workable plot from those sparks.

Setting

Sometimes story ideas come from a place. A haunted house, the bayou, a colony off Jupiter. Some location captures your imagination and you just can't shake it. But you also have no clue what happens in that place. Since all plots need conflict, a good place to start is to look at the possible problems that setting or place has to offer.

1. What are the inherent dangers of this setting?
2. What are typical problems found in this setting?
3. Are there any past disasters connected to this setting?
4. How could someone use this setting to their advantage?

The dangers of the setting might provide natural problems for your protagonist to overcome. They can also be things an antagonist might be trying to work with for some fiendish purpose. Here's a quick example using the haunted house setting:

1. **What are the inherent dangers of this setting?** Ghosts who want revenge
2. **What are typical problems found in this setting?** Local kids trespass, daring each other to stay the night
3. **Are there any past disasters connected to this setting?** The murders that spawned the ghosts, missing kids who stayed the night and never came out of the house.
4. **How could someone use this setting to their advantage?** Criminal on the run wants to hide in the house to escape the police.

See how easily a plot is unfolding here? You could take these four details and write a book about a cop who's trying to find some missing kids, goes into this haunted house, and gets into trouble with both the criminal and the ghosts. All it took was a few minutes of brainstorming about the setting.

Event or Situation

Sometimes the idea is a situation or event: a sun going supernova; a threat to a place or person, like a kidnapped child or a terrorist attack; discovery of something profound, either personal or for the world. Something is happening or about to happen, and someone is going to have to deal with it in some way. Questions you might ask here are:

1. Who has the most to lose in this situation?
2. Who has the most to gain in this situation?
3. Who has the freedom to act, but is also restricted in some way?
4. Who can be hurt the most from this situation?
5. What must be done to resolve this situation?

Situation plots usually need the most work on the character goals and stakes, because we know the what, but not the who or why. It's easy to find surface goals and stakes (to save the word, to stop the bad guy, save a life), but you often find that those aren't deep enough to help you create the plot. You run out of problems for the protagonist to tackle pretty quickly. The trick is to find the personal stakes and then work from there to determine the goals. People act when they want to (something to gain) or *have* to (something to lose).

Personal Journey

Journeys are common in character-driven and literary novels, and even in fantasies. A woman tries to find herself after a failed marriage. A man takes to the sea to live the last months of his life after being diagnosed with a terminal illness. A group of adventurers goes on quest for an item of importance. The journey is what matters most, not what's found on the other side. Some things to think about here are:

1. What are the inherent dangers of this journey?
2. What are the inherent joys of this journey?

3. What resistance would someone get from friends regarding this journey?
4. What fears would keep someone from attempting this journey?

Character growth is key in a story like this, as the journey is almost always what allows them to find what they're looking for. To grow, the protagonist needs to overcome personal issues that were holding them back. They need to learn ways to better themselves and put them to use. Goals are just as important as in any other story, but they'll often be more personal and internal rather than external. The external obstacles are the ways in which the lesson is learned.

Premise or Idea

A what if? idea is a common start to a story. What if someone developed magic powers? What if a mother of three had to become a thief to support her kids? What if a foreign sleeper agent actually became president? These are cool ideas that can be explored in a myriad of ways. The trick is to narrow that grand idea down to find the personal connections that will give you your protagonist.

1. How would this person/people react to this idea?
2. How would others react to them?
3. Who is personally affected by this?
4. What do they have to lose by this?
5. What can go wrong were this to happen?

Getting personal can help you figure out who your protagonist is and what they'll have to do to resolve this "what if" situation. Even epic thrillers like Tom Clancy novels have characters with personal stakes so the idea doesn't take over the story. Readers still need to care about someone before they'll care about the problem that someone faces.

Characters

Starting with a character is probably one of the most common idea generators. A girl who can shift pain; a man grieving over his dead son; a woman who reads tea leaves. You hear lots of writers talk about that voice that wouldn't stop talking to them. Take a moment and listen to what that voice has to say.

1. What does this character do that might put them in danger?
2. What terrible secret or tragic event is this character hiding?
3. What is special or unique about this character?
4. What or who will this character risk all for?
5. What do they want most?
6. What do they fear most?

Odds are if you have a character in mind, the plot will be much easier to figure out, since characters drive plot. Focus on the goals of that character. What they want, what they don't want, what they fear. Figure out what they *want* most, then put the things they *fear* most in their way.

All of these questions can help aid you in plotting, so mix and match. Put the terminally ill man on a space freighter secretly concealing a pirate with an evil plan. Let the woman who can read tea leaves try to find the missing kids last seen in a haunted house. Plots are formed when you start asking questions about what people will do and why, and what will happen if they fail.

Plot is people doing stuff to get stuff. All you have to do is figure out the stuff.

Janice Hardy offers more tips about writing on her blog, "The Other Side of the Story" (http://blog.janicehardy.com/). She's also the author of the teen fantasy trilogy The Healing Wars, where she tapped into her own dark side to create a world where healing was dangerous, and those with the best intentions often made the worst choices. Her books include *The Shifter*, *Blue Fire*, and the upcoming *Darkfall* from Balzer+Bray/Harper Collins. www.janicehardy.com

Plot: Not Just Another Word for a Hole in a Graveyard

by Jenny Milchman

We can bat about terms like "literary" versus "genre" fiction till people cease to die, but the truth is every body needs a grave, and every story needs a plot.

I can already hear the opposing cries. "No, no," they say. "What every book needs is great characters."

(And anyway, how about cremation?)

Well, yes. I agree with you. But what are great characters supposed to *do*? Therein lies your plot.

But how exactly do you construct a plot?

Here's one method, with much of the credit going to that great genius of story, Robert McKee. His book — *Story* — is worth more than a look. For now I'm going to piece together McKee's wisdom with some of what I've learned myself, then challenge each of you to create the bare bones of a terrific new plot.

Each story has to have a start, of course. The *inciting incident* kicks things off, just as the first kick of a football game sets the players on a course to win or lose. If you come up with a toothsome inciting incident, your plot will be off to a great start.

Think of scenarios that intrigue you. Did you ever get stopped in traffic so thick you couldn't see its source — then start wondering about that source? A terrible accident maybe? A broken down bus? (There's just something inherently dramatic about a bus....) Or possibly a driver so sick of things he left behind his car?

Or perhaps your telephone just rang late at night. Before you pick it up to learn that your daughter got scared at her sleepover and wants to come home, let your imagination run a little bit wild, let your heart start pounding. You will have the makings of an inciting incident.

After the inciting incident is set up, and the characters needed to fulfill it are introduced, with its ramification played out a bit, you come to **plot point 1**. This occurs at roughly 1/3 of the way through your story. Plot point 1 takes what you have begun to create and sends it careening off in a new direction.

Maybe the driver did leave behind his car — but now he comes back. Or perhaps when you get to the sleepover…nobody's home.

About another third of the way through your story comes, what else? **Plot point 2**. Again, your story is going to be turned somehow, sent off in another direction. If you think about the story as a steadily rising arc, the plot points are forks along it. The action continues to rise, but it's not a straight progression.

All the scenes and moments you have created so far call for an awakening at this point in the story. You don't want things to be linear — you want to introduce the unexpected. Think about the least likely thing that could happen. Then think about the most likely thing. Something somewhere in-between will be a great plot point. If all else fails, you can have someone knock on the door. Even if this plot point doesn't stand in the final version, it will get you moving towards something new.

Plot point 2 leads into the **climax** of your story. This is where all the scenes, threads, and characters you have arrayed come together in one knotted ball of action, only to be swiftly unraveled during the **denouement** so the reader can have a moment of quietude and rest — just before dashing to his or her computer.

Why will he or she dash there?

Because your now loyal reader wants to see if you have any other books — trusting you completely to deliver a well-constructed, seamless plot.

Jenny Milchman is a suspense writer from New Jersey. She is founder of the series Writing Matters, which draws authors and publishing professionals from both coasts to standing-room-only events at a local bookstore. In 2010 she created Take Your Child to a Bookstore Day, a holiday that went viral, enlisting booksellers in 30 states, two Canadian provinces, and England. Jenny is the author of the short story "The Very Old Man," an Amazon bestseller in mystery anthologies. Another short story will be published in 2012 in a book called Adirondack Mysteries II. Her novel, a literary thriller titled *Cover of Snow*, is forthcoming from Ballantine. www.jennymilchman.com

Plotting by the Seat of Your Pants

by Susanne Alleyn

They say there are two types of fiction writers: plotters and pantsers.

Plotters are blessed with the ability to create complex plots from beginning to end; they write down a complete outline, whether in a loose synopsis, a tightly structured timeline, a series of index cards, or whatever, before they write Word One of the actual novel. Pantsers, on the other hand, can't possibly think that far ahead, and take an idea, a situation, a setting, a character or two, with a rough idea of where the story is going, and just plunge onward, writing "by the seat of their pants."

There are advantages to both of these methods, and which method works for you depends on what kind of writer (and basic personality) you are. I, for one, am a pantser. I write mysteries, among other things, and I couldn't come up with the entire outline of a novel, particularly a mystery novel, even if you held a gun to my head. But if I begin with a basic idea, if I know how my story begins (who got murdered) and how it ends (whodunnit and why), then I trust my subconscious to come up with the dreaded middle of the story as I move... OK, feel my way blindly... forward.

Are there disadvantages to this method? Sure. It's probably slower. I'm sure it takes longer for me to write a novel, working this way, than it takes someone who has carefully plotted out her novel ahead of time. But the advantages, I've found, are that the novel grows more or less naturally as I proceed. At the risk of sounding like a pretentious literary critic, the development of the plot is more "organic" than it would be if I tried to work out a plot and force events to happen the way I think they should happen, or want them to happen for my own storytelling convenience.

By starting my novel at Point A, without much knowledge of how I'll get past Points B through Y before successfully arriving at the end (Point Z), somehow the plot manages to create itself without too much goading from me. The situation or character I might suddenly come up with for Point E in the story eventually creates an idea for Point J or K, which leads to Points L and M, and so on.

An example of how the sneaky old subconscious can work? Three years ago, I was writing the first draft of *The Cavalier of the Apocalypse*, a historical mystery set in prerevolutionary Paris. All I had, at the start, was an idea that the murder would be connected somehow to the famous (real-life) Diamond Necklace Affair of 1785-86, and to the (now two-century-old) conspiracy theory that the Freemasons were involved in the scandal, with the goal of bringing down the French monarchy.

While toiling my way through the first quarter of the novel (not yet knowing how the heck I was going to unmask my killer), I sent my sleuth, Aristide Ravel, with the dead man's waistcoat to a fashionable tailor, in hopes of identifying the corpse. The tailor gave him half a dozen names of customers who had had identical waistcoats made; the dead man was sure to be one of them. I already knew which one he was, and where he lived, and how the next scene would play out when, after a dead end or two, Ravel interviewed his family.

And at this point (perhaps I'd reached Point F or G), I still didn't have the faintest idea how the story was going to play itself out, or how I was going to keep the solution to the mystery from being ridiculously obvious, although I thought I knew who'd committed the murder. And I'd also begun to realize that, unless I wanted it to be a very short novel, something else (anything!) had to happen under mysterious circumstances to complicate things.

But (spoilers ahead) for some reason, one of the names on the tailor's list suddenly became a fully-fleshed character, a Freemason with fishy connections, and very quickly developed a personality. He walked into the story, took over, stole the corpse, and dragged the plot off in another direction entirely.

Where did he come from? I haven't the slightest idea, beyond "somewhere in the back of my subconscious mind." Then, because he existed, another character also had to appear, and he rapidly became one of the major characters in the novel. At last it became suddenly quite obvious to me that this second character was actually the murderer, and since he was a great improvement over my original choice of killer, I let him have the role. And when I went back to (minimally) revise all the chapters I'd already completed, in order to accommodate him, the clues I'd laid out worked much, much better for the new killer than for the old.

Wow.

I'd always thought writers were being a bit affected when they talked about characters taking over their stories, but, boy, this was one time when I saw it happen in front of me. And the story developed, and the characters evolved, and, gosh darn it, it worked.

So if you're a plotter, if you have more detailed, perfectly constructed stories whirling around in your brain than you'll ever have time to set down, if you adore outlining your novels, go right ahead. If you absolutely need to know exactly how your story will unfold, chapter by chapter, before you start writing the narrative, go right ahead.

But if someone has told you that you should outline, synopsize, or otherwise rigidly structure your novel before starting to write it, and you just don't feel comfortable or happy doing that (or if trying to come up with the next damn plot point in your synopsis feels like having all your teeth pulled out, one by one, without Novocain), then ignore the advice. You're probably a pantser.

Take your basic starter idea and run with it. Start at Point A, with an idea of Point B, go there, write a scene, create a new character, and discover to what sort of Point C your Point B may lead you. Throw in extra stuff in the course of dialogues or descriptions or minor characters (you can always edit out the excess — the padding and the bits that don't lead you anywhere — later). The smallest detail in a scene you write may suddenly, as your subconscious works, turn into something that drives your plot.

Eventually you'll reach Point Z, which may or may not be the Point Z you imagined a while ago, if you ever had a firm idea in the first place about how your novel was going to end. And the bonus is that your new ending may very well be heaps better than your original ending, because it's grown organically (there's that word again) in your writer's subconscious from everything that has gone before. So sit back and let the subconscious and the seat of the pants take over!

Susanne Alleyn is the author of the Aristide Ravel French Revolution mystery series (*The Cavalier of the Apocalypse*, *Palace of Justice*, *Game of Patience*, and *A Treasury of Regrets*), and of *A Far Better Rest*, a re-imagining of *A Tale of Two Cities*. She is the granddaughter of children's author Lillie V. Albrecht, who penned the classic *Deborah Remembers* (1959) and four other historical children's books, all soon to reappear as e-books. www.susannealleyn.com

Characters in Conflict

by Chris Eboch

A strong story needs conflict. But conflict doesn't just come from dramatic things happening. It comes from the character — what he or she needs and wants, and why he or she can't get it easily.

Let's start with a premise for a short story for children: a kid has a math test on Monday. Exciting? Not really. But ask two simple questions, and you can add conflict.

- Why is it important to the character? The stakes should be high. The longer the story or novel, the higher stakes you need to sustain it. A short story character might want to win a contest; a novel character might need to save the world.
- Why is it difficult for the character? Difficulties can be divided into three general categories, traditionally called man versus man, man versus nature, and man versus himself. You can even have a combination of these. For example, someone may be trying to spy on some bank robbers (man versus man) during a dangerous storm (man versus nature) when he is afraid of lightning (man versus himself).

For our kid with the math test, here's one example: It's important because if he doesn't pass, he'll fail the class, have to go to summer school, and not get to go to football camp, when football is what he loves most. Assuming we create a character readers like, they'll care about the outcome of this test and root for him to succeed.

Our football lover could have lots of challenges — he forgot his study book, he's expected to baby-sit, a storm knocked out the power, he has ADHD, or he suffers test anxiety. But ideally we'll relate the difficulty to the reason it's important. So let's say he has a game Sunday afternoon and is getting pressure from his coach and teammates to practice rather than study. Plus, he'd rather play football anyway.

We now have a situation full of potential tension. Let the character struggle enough before he succeeds (or fails and learns a lesson), and you'll have a story. And if these two questions can pump up a dull premise, just think what they can do with an exciting one!

Fears and Desires

As this exercise shows, conflict doesn't just come from the plot. It comes from the interaction between character and plot. You can create conflict by setting up situations which force a person to confront their fears. If someone is afraid of heights, make them go someplace high. If they're afraid of taking responsibility, force them to be in charge.

You can also create conflict by setting up situations that oppose a person's desires. Sometimes these desires are for practical things. In my middle grade mystery set in ancient Egypt, *The Eyes of Pharaoh*, the main character is a young temple dancer whose one goal is to win an upcoming contest. When her friend disappears, she has to decide if winning the contest is really more important than helping a friend.

A character's desires can also be more general, related to the way they want to live. In my adult romantic suspense novel, *Rattled* (written as Kris Bock), Erin likes her adventures safely in books. But when she finds a clue to a century-old lost treasure, she's thrust into a wilderness expedition full of dangers from wild animals, nasty humans, and nature itself. If you have a character who craves safety, put her in danger. But if she craves danger, keep her out of it.

Perhaps your character simply wants an ordinary life. In my Mayan historical novel *The Well of Sacrifice*, Eveningstar never dreams of being a leader or a rebel. But when her family, the government, and even the gods fail to stop the evil high priest who is trying to take over the city, she's forced to act. The reluctant hero is a staple of books and movies because it's fun to watch someone forced into a heroic role when they don't want it. (Think of Han Solo in *Star Wars*.)

Even with nonfiction, you can create tension by focusing on the challenges that make a person's accomplishments more impressive. In *Jesse Owens: Young Record Breaker* (written under the name M. M. Eboch), I made this incredible athlete's story more powerful by focusing on all the things he had to overcome — not just racism, but also childhood health problems, poverty, and a poor education. I showed his successes *and* his troubles, to help the reader understand what he achieved.

Some writers start with plot ideas and then develop the character who'll face those challenges, while others start with a great character and then figure out what he or she does. Regardless, remember to work back and forth between plot and character, tying them together with conflict.

Additional notes on Building Characters

Create conflict by setting up situations which oppose a person's needs. Six basic human needs influence character:

1. Security (knowing the future)

2. Change (desire for variety, excitement)

3. Connection (feeling part of a group)

4. Independence (personal identity/freedom)

5. Growth (working toward a personal goal)

6. Contribution (feeling needed, worthwhile)

-   What statements of self would they use? ("I always...I never...I'm the kind of person who....") If these are true, a situation that challenges that will create conflict. If these statements are false, a situation that exposes that will create conflict.

-   Heroes should be realistic, complex and individual. Make sure your heroes have flaws. Characters should have a mix of traits, good and bad, sometimes working against each other (such as bright but undisciplined). Even the people you love have flaws and irritating quirks. So should your characters. Think of unusual/contradictory qualities for all characters (a tough bully who loves gerbils).

-   Heroes should have universal traits (emotions and motives). Readers should identify/sympathize to some extent, so they'll forgive the main character for their mistakes.

-   Your hero should have the qualities needed to realistically overcome the challenge. Thus, the challenges should be hard enough to be dramatic (we must believe the hero could fail), yet not so great that no real person could solve them.

- In general, the protagonist should grow and change in the course of the story. She should make errors and learn something. Heroes need both inner and outer challenges.

- Protagonists should be active, not passive. They should take risks and accept responsibility. They may be at least partly responsible for their own problems. They should have to sacrifice something in order to succeed (pride, safety, financial security).

- Heroes may be willing or unwilling. They may be outcasts, cynics, loners, wounded or reluctant. But at some point they should commit to the challenge.

- Your hero should be actively involved in solving the problem at the end. She should not simply be rescued by outside forces or luck.

- Your hero's rewards should be proportionate to the challenges.

Villains should also be well-rounded. A villain with good qualities and understandable motives creates a more subtle and complex story. Why is the villain nasty? Are they actually evil, or ignorant, or do their goals just conflict with your hero's?

Other major characters also need strengths and weaknesses. Think about their motives, their good qualities and their flaws. All your characters should have needs and wants. Put the various characters' goals in opposition to each other and you'll have enough conflict to sustain a novel.

Plotting Like a Screenwriter

by Douglas J. Eboch

Solid plotting is critical to screenwriters. Movies are expected to deliver stories with the complexity and depth of a novel but in much less time. The average screenplay is 110 pages with lots of white on the page. That means we have to be very efficient. As a result, Hollywood has developed a "three act structure" concept of plotting.

But before I get into the three act structure, I want to discuss the foundation of narrative. This may seem a little basic at first, but there is a method to my madness. I want to show that the three act approach is not some Hollywood formula but grows out of the fundamental nature of storytelling.

So let me start by addressing the question: What is a story?

A story needs three things. First, we need a character. The character need not be human, but he or she must behave in recognizably human fashion — Mickey Mouse, for example. If you don't have a character you may be writing a travel guide, op-ed essay, or a scientific treatise but you are not writing a story.

Next, the character must be facing some kind of dilemma. I don't really care to hear about someone whose life is just fine. I mean, that's great for them, but how does it affect me? Whatever it is that causes us to respond to made-up stories has something to do with watching how people deal with problems.

Finally, a story needs a resolution. I'm watching/listening/reading to find out how this character deals with their problem. I'm not going to be satisfied until I see how it all comes out.

If you have those three things, you have a story — even a thirty-second narrative commercial has them. A young man (character) is not getting good gas mileage (dilemma) so he tries a different type of gasoline and his mileage improves (resolution).

But simply having a character, dilemma, and resolution doesn't necessarily make the story dramatic. If you have a guy sitting in his living room whose dilemma is that he's hungry and he goes into the kitchen to make a sandwich you have a story…but not a very dramatic one.

There are two things that affect how dramatic your story is: stakes and obstacles. The more that's at stake for the character and the greater the obstacles standing in the way of successfully resolving the dilemma, the more dramatic your story becomes. Of course "dramatic" isn't quite the same as "good" but we'll get to that.

Those five things — character, dilemma, resolution, stakes and obstacles — are the basis of three-act structure. In act one we introduce a character with a dilemma and show what's at stake. In act two the character tries to resolve their dilemma but faces increasing obstacles. And in act three we get some kind of resolution (not necessarily successful, but final.)

Now let's look at the components of three act structure. Probably the most important is the Dramatic Question. If you understand nothing else but the Dramatic Question and the Moment of Failure (which I'll get to in a bit) you'll probably end up with a fairly well structured story.

What the Dramatic Question Is

The Dramatic Question is the structural spine of your story. On some level all Dramatic Questions can be boiled down to "Will the character solve their dilemma?" Of course that's not very helpful to the writer trying to crack a particular story. You need to ask that question with the specifics of your character and dilemma.

So in *Star Wars* (written by George Lucas) the question is "Will Luke Skywalker defeat Darth Vadar?" In *E.T. The Extra-Terrestrial* (written by Melissa Mathison) it's "Can Elliot save E.T.?" In *Little Miss Sunshine* (written by Michael Arndt) it's "Will Olive win the beauty pageant?"

Those sound simple, right? Simpler is better when it comes to the Dramatic Question. But it's not always easy to be simple. You have to know who your character is and what their dilemma is before you can craft a nice simple Dramatic Question. But then if you haven't figured out your character and their dilemma, you're not really ready to start writing yet anyway!

I also think it's good to phrase the Dramatic Question as a yes or no question. So it's not "Who will Susan marry?" it's "Will Susan marry Bill?" Keeping it yes/no helps you tightly focus your narrative.

What the Dramatic Question Is Not

The Dramatic Question is not the theme of your movie. It's not the hook. It's not necessarily the character arc (sometimes it is, but not usually.) It doesn't define whether your story is sophisticated or facile.

Do not think the Dramatic Question determines the quality of your story. It's simply the spine on which you're going to build your story. What you hang on that spine is going to determine how good your script is. Just because a person doesn't collapse under the weight of their own body doesn't mean they're beautiful, intelligent, interesting, or emotionally complex. However, if your spine isn't solid, none of the other stuff is going to work properly either.

How to use the Dramatic Question in your story

The Dramatic Question is an unspoken agreement with the audience. It tells them what the scope and shape of the story is going to be. They need to know what the question is fairly early in the proceedings or you will lose them. If too much time passes before they understand the Dramatic Question they're liable to walk out of the theater or turn the DVD off or put down your script. They'll say something like, "I couldn't figure out what the movie was about."

The moment when the Dramatic Question becomes clear is called the Catalyst. The Catalyst is where the audience understands who the main character is and what their basic dilemma is. They may not understand the entire dimension of the problem, but they have an idea what the story arc will be about.

So in *E.T.* the catalyst is when Elliot sees E.T. for the first time. We don't yet know that his mission will ultimately be to get E.T. home or even that first he'll have to hide E.T. And we don't know that E.T. will start dying from the Earth environment. But we know that this kid who nobody takes seriously just found a little lost alien — and that some scary men are looking for it. We have a character with a dilemma.

Similarly, when the audience knows the outcome of the Dramatic Question, your story is over. The audience will stick with you for a few minutes of wrap up, but if you go on too long after resolving the dramatic question, they're going to get restless. They'll say things like, "it was anti-climactic" or "it had too many endings."

Once E.T. takes off in his space ship, the movie ends. Credits roll. The story is over. Compare that to the *Lord of the Rings* trilogy (screenplay by Fran Walsh & Philippa Boyens & Peter Jackson). The Dramatic Question is "Can Frodo destroy the ring?" He does, but then the movie continues for another forty minutes or so. Kind of got tedious didn't it? The story was over. We wanted to go home.

The structural beat where you answer the Dramatic Question is called the Resolution.

Apparent Failure/Success

There's one other critical structural concept you need to understand. That is the moment of apparent failure (or success). Whatever the Resolution to your Dramatic Question is, there needs to be a moment where the opposite appears to be inevitable. If your character succeeds at the end, you need a moment where it appears the character must fail. And if your character fails at the end, you need a moment where they appear about to succeed.

This moment should come late in the story as the tension is building toward the climax. We need it so the audience can't predict how the movie's going to unfold. We may know that in a big Hollywood movie the hero will beat the bad guy and get the girl, but we shouldn't be able to figure out how they'll accomplish that. In screenwriting, we call this moment of apparent failure/success the Act Two Break.

Breaking Your Story into Three Acts

Now let's discuss how you apply the three act structure to your story. It might be useful if I first point out that there are no actual act breaks in a movie. A movie is a continuous experience. In a play there often are act breaks — the curtain comes down, the lights come up and the audience goes out to the lobby for a drink. In TV there are act breaks that are filled by commercials. But in feature films there are no actual breaks in the narrative.

Instead, when we say "act break," we're talking about a literary concept. We use act breaks to discuss critical turning points in the story. Since this is a literary concept it can be subjective. You and I might disagree on the act breaks in a given story. There's no way to tell who's right and who's wrong. As a writer you identify the act breaks in the way that is most useful to you in telling your story.

So, we have our Dramatic Question that is introduced in the Catalyst and answered in the Resolution. Typically, the Catalyst comes around page ten of your screenplay. The Resolution should probably come in the last six to eight pages. That leaves a lot of pages in between. We could use some structural landmarks to help us out.

As I said earlier, the first act is the section of your story where you introduce your character, their dilemma, and what's at stake. This typically takes up the first fourth of your screenplay. Sometime around page twenty-five or thirty there will be an act break — The First Act Break. This is the point at which your character embarks on the journey of the movie, sometimes known as the "point of no return."

The second act takes up roughly the middle half of your screenplay. This is where the character tries to solve their problem but faces escalating obstacles and, ideally, escalating stakes. It ends at the Second Act Break, which I've already mentioned is the point of apparent success or failure.

The third act, then, takes up roughly the last quarter of your screenplay. It provides the climactic resolution to your story.

So now let's look at the major signposts of the three act structure in order, adding a few other beats to help keep things moving:

Status Quo

Generally you want to spend a little time showing the character in their status quo before introducing the catalyst of the story. We need to get to know who the character is so we can understand how the story changes them.

For example, in *E.T.* we see Elliot at home. His parents are divorced and his father has moved out. His older brother and his friends are playing a game. Elliot wants to play, but they won't let him. And when he claims something strange is out in the shed, nobody takes him seriously. He's longing to fit in but ignored.

It's usually best if you show the most interesting part of your character's status quo, not the most boring. We meet Indiana Jones escaping traps, traitorous assistants and angry tribesmen — not doing his laundry! This is why it's usually not a good idea to open your movie with your character waking up in the morning — that's seldom the most interesting part of someone's day.

The Catalyst

The Catalyst is the point at which the main character and their dilemma are made clear to the audience. It's when the Dramatic Question gets asked. So in *Little Miss Sunshine* the catalyst is when we learn that Olive has gotten into the pageant, but it's in Los Angeles in a couple days. Now interestingly, the main character of this movie is the father, Richard. He's the one whose decisions are driving the action. But the Dramatic Question centers on Olive: Will she win the pageant? In this case Richard's goal is to help his daughter be a winner.

In *Star Wars*, the catalyst is when Luke Skywalker sees R2D2 project the hologram of Princess Leia and decides he wants to help her. The audience knows that Leia is being held by Darth Vadar and that Vadar is looking for R2D2. The Dramatic Question becomes, "Will Luke beat Darth Vadar?" Note that Luke doesn't even know about Vadar yet and that the audience doesn't know the Death Star will eventually come to threaten the rebel base. We don't need all these details, we simply need to understand what the core of the story is going to be about. We know Luke has a dilemma even if he doesn't!

Act One Break

The Act One Break is the point at which the character actually embarks on the journey of the story. It's sometimes known as the "point of no return." I think that's a good way to look at it — from here on out the character has no choice but to see this through to the end. If the character can walk away from the story without losing anything there isn't much tension. At the Act One Break you have to trap them in the story.

The Act One Break in *Little Miss Sunshine* is when the family sets out on their road trip to California. In *Star Wars* the Act One Break is when Luke goes with Obi Wan to Mos Eisley to find a pilot to take them into space. The Act One Break in *E.T.* is when Elliot first feels E.T.'s feelings when E.T. is scared by an umbrella. At that point E.T. and Elliot are linked. If Elliot doesn't help the little alien, there are going to be serious consequences for him.

In all these cases, if the character walks away from the story after this point they will fail in their goal and suffer for it. They are locked in.

Midpoint

As you might expect, the Midpoint is a beat that occurs in the middle of the movie, which also makes it the middle of Act Two. The concept of the Midpoint is fairly straightforward, though its use and purpose can vary a lot. I know several successful screenwriters who don't give any thought to the midpoint and I've seen movies that don't have a traditional midpoint. It doesn't really seem to be a required beat. But it can be a valuable milestone to help us keep things moving. If used well, it can be the tent pole that supports Act Two.

Traditionally the Midpoint mirrors the Resolution and is opposite to the Act Two Break. If your character is going to succeed at their goal in the Resolution, then the Midpoint should be a moment of success and the Act

Two Break will be a moment of failure. If the character will fail in the Resolution, then the Midpoint will be a moment of failure and the Act Two Break a moment of success. In this way we'll have a story that has dramatic peaks and valleys.

So in *Star Wars*, the midpoint is Luke rescuing Princess Leia from the prison cell. It's a moment of success in a movie where ultimately Luke will succeed in defeating Darth Vadar.

In *Little Miss Sunshine* Olive actually fails to win the pageant at the resolution. Though the movie has a "happy" ending emotionally, in terms of the Dramatic Question Richard is ultimately unsuccessful. The Act Two Break is when the family finally arrives at the pageant and Richard manages to get registered in the nick of time — a moment of success. The Midpoint, then, is when Grandpa dies, a big setback that mirrors the resolution.

The Midpoint often twists the story in a new direction or adds a new element. It's also a good place to raise the stakes. In *E.T.* the Midpoint is when E.T. figures out his plan to "phone home," but it's also the point when they first realize E.T. and Eliot are getting sick. So we both add a new element — the plan — and increase the consequences of failure.

The Act Two Break

The Act Two Break is one of the most critical beats of your story. It's often referred to as the "lowest moment," though I don't like that because I think it's misleading. Seldom do I see a successful story where things start getting better right after the Act Two Break. I think "moment of greatest failure" is a better description. It's also sometimes called the "all is lost" moment, which is pretty good. The point is that this is when it looks like your character is doomed to fail. The Act Two Break in *E.T.* is E.T. apparently dying and the breaking of the psychic link with Elliot.

That assumes, of course, that ultimately your character will succeed. Some stories, like *Little Miss Sunshine*, end with the character failing in their goal, and in this case you have to reverse the Act Two Break. It becomes the moment of greatest success. Gangster movies often work this way — the gangster seizes control of the gang at the end of Act Two and looks like he'll be unstoppable. But by the end he'll be lying dead in the street, riddled with bullets.

Why is this so important? Because the ending won't be satisfying unless it's hard to achieve. And you don't want your movie to feel completely predictable. This is the point where the audience needs to think, "Boy, I know the hero must be going to beat the bad guy and get the girl (this is a movie, after all), but I sure don't know how he's going to do it. It seems hopeless."

Hope and fear come into play here. What is the audience rooting for? Do they want the character to succeed or fail? (Both are possibilities depending on your premise.) This is the moment where you make them think the opposite might actually happen. Or in a tragedy you make them think they might get the ending they want, only to snatch it away from them. Romeo and Juliet hatch a plan to run away together… maybe it will all work out after all….

The Act Two Break in *Star Wars* is when our heroes escape the Death Star in the Millennium Falcon… but we learn that Darth Vadar has put a tracking device on their ship. It's their biggest failure because they're going to lead the bad guys right to the rebel base.

The Epiphany

When the character has really hit rock bottom (or the height of their success), that's when the Epiphany comes. This is the twist that shows us how the character is going to succeed (or fail) after all. In *Star Wars* the Epiphany is the briefing scene when the general explains the weakness in the Death Star. Luke now knows how he can beat Darth Vader. Most often the character themselves has the realization, but sometimes the character has already figured it out and it's the audience who's let in on the secret.

It's important here that you avoid the Deus Ex Machina ending. This is an ending where some outside force saves the day for the character. The term comes from Aristotle and means literally "God in the Machine," referring to those ancient plays where an actor playing Zeus would be lowered in a basket to sort everything out for the characters. A more modern equivalent would be the cavalry to the rescue in a western. Endings where the character succeeds by pure luck also fall into this category.

To avoid this, the Epiphany must be set up. Whatever realization the character has must be planted, usually around the midpoint. We know Princess Leia has put something into R2D2. Luke has rescued Leia and brought her and the 'droid back to the rebels. When it is revealed that the robot contains the Death Star plans and that these reveal a weakness, it feels organic because the elements have been planted and Luke was critical to bringing them together. But the audience was kept in the dark just enough so that they didn't know how this twist would come about.

In *Little Miss Sunshine,* the epiphany is when Richard realizes he loves Olive more than he cares about winning. He wants to stop her from competing in the pageant for fear she'll be humiliated. He hasn't quite figured out how he's going to succeed (Olive does compete) but he's had the key realization he needs for the Resolution.

In *E.T.,* the epiphany is when Elliot realizes E.T. isn't actually dead and they've succeeded in contacting his people after all. This may seem a bit convenient, but notice that Elliot is far from done here. He now has to get E.T. out of the heavily guarded house and to the landing site. He knows *how* to succeed, but he still has to do it.

The Resolution

The Resolution is the climax of the movie. It should be big and exciting and emotional. It is also the moment when the Dramatic Question is answered either positively or negatively. Thus, it is what we've been waiting for since the Catalyst.

In addition to making this a big moment, it is crucial that you make it a final moment. The Dramatic Question must be answered definitively. If our hero can just go out and try again, then we don't feel like the question is resolved. The Resolution must be the last chance for success or failure. If Luke can't destroy the Death Star, then the rebellion will be crushed. It's not just another battle; it's the climactic battle.

The resolution is usually pretty obvious. Luke destroys the Death Star. E.T. gets to the spaceship. In *Little Miss Sunshine*, Richard gets up onstage with Olive and dances with her in support, and in defiance of the pageant people who want Olive off the stage. Olive may lose the pageant, answering the Dramatic Question in the negative, but the previously dysfunctional family has come together.

These are the structural stages Hollywood screenwriters use to build well-plotted scripts. Of course, a well-structured script isn't the same as a good script. You still have to write the actual characters and scenes. But if you have a strong plot, then you have a solid foundation that will allow you to tell a truly great story.

Douglas J. Eboch wrote the original script for the movie *Sweet Home Alabama.* He teaches at Art Center College of Design and lectures internationally. He also writes a blog about screenwriting, where he shares techniques like the ones in this article: http://letsschmooze.blogspot.com/.

Plot Turning Points

by Janet Fox

Traditional plots contain *turning points*, or transition points — points in the plot at which your protagonist's problem-solving action turns in a new direction. Turning points are important because they serve to increase tension and thus reader interest.

Put it this way: turning points are the significant moments of change in your story.

Beginning with Aristotle, who defined three-act structure, a number of writers and critics have identified these points and where they usually occur in the plot and given them names and relative value. There are seven especially important turning points. In order of appearance they are: *the inciting incident; plot point one; pinch one; midpoint; crisis; plot point two; climax.*

Before I discuss where these turning points occur in the plot, I'd like to explain what I mean by how the protagonist's action "turns." Your protagonist has an identifiable goal and must surmount a number of increasingly difficult obstacles. Each time she thinks she's closing in on her goal, some new obstacle arises and forces her to "turn" to a new method of solving her problem. Until the climax of the story, she is unable to resolve the problem, and with each turn the stakes are raised.

Furthermore, in the first half of traditional plot structure, your protagonist makes poor choices and her actions serve to turn the situation for the worse. In the second half of your story, your protagonist has begun to learn from her mistakes and although she can't solve the problem until the climax, her actions turn the situation for the better.

For example, in my second young adult novel, *Forgiven*, Kula initially makes poor choices born out of her ignorance and stubbornness. She denies her father, which forces her to go to San Francisco; upon arriving in San Francisco she lets the coach driver dupe her and ends up in the notorious Barbary Coast; she goes into Chinatown after being repeatedly told to avoid it and ends up in danger; she falls for charming Will Henderson and spills secrets she ought to keep. Each action comes at a turning point in the novel and both raises the stakes for Kula and increases the tension. In the second half of the novel the turning points still raise the stakes, but Kula is now taking actions born out of determination (the positive side of stubbornness) as she learns.

Let's take each turning point in order, define each, and see where each one should place in a novel's plot.

In order to picture where turning points place, note that in 3-act structure Act I and Act III are roughly the same length while Act II is twice as long as either of the other acts. Draw a line and divide it accordingly, and put points on this line for each turning point.

The *inciting incident* should occur right up front. In a longer novel it might occur within the first chapter; often it occurs within the first few pages. The inciting incident is the incident that kick-starts the forward motion of the story; after the inciting incident your protagonist has no choice; she must act. Example: In Suzanne Collins' *The Hunger Games*, the inciting incident is the reaping that forces Katniss to take the place of her beloved sister Prim.

Plot point one occurs at the transition between Act I and Act II. Plot point one is the true beginning of the story, the point of no return for the protagonist. Example: In *Forgiven*, it's the moment when Kula leaves Montana for San Francisco, for she has no choice if she is to save her dad.

Pinch one occurs halfway between plot point one and the midpoint (the actual middle of the novel.) A pinch is a lesser turning point; it has significance but is not as huge as the other turning points. Example: In *Forgiven*, Kula learns that the box she seeks is in the hands of the antagonist; she resolves to find the box by questioning the antagonist's girlfriend.

The *midpoint* is just that, smack in the middle of Act II, but it is also a turning point of high value. It is the moment when the protagonist changes from making one mistake after another to learning and adapting. She may not have achieved her goal, but now she's getting things done. Example: In *The Hunger Games*, Katniss realizes that Peeta has saved her life, that he loves her and would sacrifice himself for her; it's the beginning of her realization of the importance of their relationship, and the realization that she would also sacrifice for him.

The *crisis* is halfway between the midpoint and plot point two. The crisis is a true high point of drama, a moment of supreme tension. It can be a "near-death experience." Example: In *The Hunger Games*, Katniss's one true friend (and a stand-in for Prim) Rue dies. This solidifies Katniss's full resolve to win the Games.

Plot point two occurs at the transition from Act II to Act III. Its value is less than that of the crisis and midpoint, but it still signals a change. Act II is the "realm of the antagonist" — the arena in which the antagonist dominates — and by Act III the antagonist may not be finished but is certainly in decline. Plot point two turns the action in favor of the protagonist. Example: In *Forgiven*, the earthquake occurs at plot point two. Kula must now pool all her resources — especially her determination — to survive and to help those around her.

The *climax* is the moment of ultimate resolution: defeat of the antagonist; the protagonist has won the day and achieved her goal, even if at high cost; it is also called the obligatory scene. It is a moment of the very highest tension and drama and comes close to the end of the novel. After the climax, there's no need to hang around the plot except to tie up remaining loose ends. Example: In *The Hunger Games* Katniss and Peeta both survive their ordeal by recognizing that they care for one another, and strategizing a solution. This climax is less than thirty pages from the end of a 374-page novel.

When I finish my first drafts I use a plot chart to see whether I've placed these seven turning points roughly where they should be according to page count. (Let me emphasize the word "roughly." A plot template should be used to help guide you, not constrain you.) I divide my manuscript into the three acts and then note where the turning points should be by page count. I also note whether their relative values are correct — if plot point two has higher tension and drama than my climax, I'd better revise.

The thing to keep in mind is that all major points in your plot should be characterized by change. Change in your protagonist is what generates tension and thus holds reader interest. And engaging reader interest is your first goal, always.

Optional exercise: Take a picture book (I like *Where The Wild Things Are*) and try to find these seven turning points in the plot. See if they fit the template in terms of page count, value, etc.

Janet Fox writes fiction and non-fiction for children of all ages including the award-winning *Get Organized Without Losing It* and the young adult novel *Faithful* (Speak/Penguin, 2010), an Amelia Bloomer List pick. Her most recent work for young adults, the historical novel *Forgiven* (June 2011; Speak/Penguin), is a 2011 Junior Library Guild selection. She lives with her husband in Bozeman, Montana. www.janetsfox.com

Add More Meat to Your Manuscript

by Chris Eboch

"I love it," the editor said. "I want to buy it." There was just one little problem. I had a 90-page manuscript for a middle grade series. He wanted 160 pages, to fit their series format for that age. "Send me the chapter by chapter synopsis on how you will rework it by next week," he said.

Of course I said, "Of course." I wasn't going to miss this chance to sell a whole series. But the manuscript already had a plot that worked well, with all the necessary elements. I wanted to keep the action-packed fast pace. How could I add 70 more pages, without getting repetitive or adding fluff that would slow the story?

Many writers wind up with long early drafts that need to be cut. But sometimes a manuscript needs to grow longer, to fit the market. A novella might have a better chance of selling as a novel. A short novel might increase in value if it's fat enough to distract the reader for several hours. Work-for-hire books often have to come in at a specific word count. And then you have cases like mine, where even an original novel needs to fit a standard series format.

I studied books on plotting, including *Beginnings, Middles, and Endings* (Nancy Kress, Elements of Fiction Writing series, Writers Digest Books) and came up with the following possibilities for filling my novel with more substance.

Add Plot

In my Haunted series, a brother and sister travel with a ghost hunter TV show and discover the girl can see ghosts. Once they figure out each ghost's story, they try to help her or him. In the original version of book 1, they find out who the ghost is quickly — the woman's name is already known, along with why she's stuck here grieving. The kids just have to discover why her husband disappeared on their wedding day. To expand the story, I forced them to do more detective work to discover the ghost's name and background.

Tip: How easily does your main character solve his problems? Can you make it more difficult, by requiring more steps or adding complications? Can you add complications to your complications, turning small steps into big challenges?

Example: In Haunted Book 2: *The Riverboat Phantom*, a ghost grabs Jon.

> *I felt the cold first on my arms, like icy vice grips squeezing my biceps. Then waves of cold flowed down to my hands, up to my shoulders, all through my body.*
> *I tried to breathe, but my chest felt too tight.*
> *My vision blurred, darkened. The last thing I saw was Tania's horrified face.*
> *And I fell.*

That's dramatic enough for a chapter ending. So what's next? It would be easiest — for Jon and the writer — if no one else notices his collapse. But if everyone notices, and Jon has to convince his worried mother that he's not sick, you get complications.

Tip: Use variations on a theme. Don't just repeat yourself — no one wants to hear the same old argument between your hero and heroine or see an identical example of your villain's villainy. But if you can add a twist, it will feel fresh. Similar scenes should also go in order from easiest to hardest challenge, or with increasing stakes, such as time running out. If your main character has already become the hero in the big game, a casual pickup game won't be compelling now — unless he has a goal other than winning.

Example: In Haunted Book 1: *The Ghost on the Stairs*, the kids make three trips to the local cemetery. The first time, they are with their mother in daylight. The second time, it's dark and stormy, and they are alone. The final time, Tania has been possessed by a ghost. Three cemetery scenes, but each different enough to feel fresh — and each scarier than the last.

Tip: Make cliffhanger endings. Cliffhanger chapter endings have the obvious advantage of driving the story forward. But they can also inspire new dramatic events. If you have to find a way to add a scary or exciting twist at the end of the chapter, the following scene automatically becomes more dramatic.

Example: In *The Ghost on the Stairs*, I originally had the kids do research in the public library. They find information, and leave, with no drama. To keep the ghost more involved, I moved their research session to the hotel's business center. That allowed me to add this dramatic chapter ending:

> *[Tania] went out. I have to admit, I was glad to be alone for awhile....*
> *It felt good to forget about ghosts and sisters and responsibilities, and just do regular stupid stuff.*
> *Then I heard the scream.*

By forcing myself to have a cliffhanger ending, I found some new and dramatic action for the next chapter. I also try to keep my chapters to no more than 1500 words for children's books, 2500 words for adult novels. If a chapter goes longer, I split it in two — which forces me to add a new cliffhanger halfway through the chapter.

Add Subplot

If you can't pack your main plot any fuller, try using subplots to add complexity and length to your manuscript. A subplot may be only loosely related to your main plot, but still add complications. A kid solving mysteries may also be distracted and inconvenienced by struggles at school, a parent dating someone new, a friend moving away, or a host of other life challenges (see the Sammy Keyes mystery novels by Wendelin Van Draanen for some great examples).

You can also think about using one or more subplots to bring out your theme. A subplot can show the other side of the story or delve into thematic ideas more deeply. If your main plot has your heroine learning to be honest in order to develop a strong romantic relationship, a subplot might show her friend lying to win a guy — and then losing him.

Tip: Can you add or expand a subplot to develop your theme? To find subplots, consider showing other aspects of your message.

Example: In the alternate reality novel *The Amethyst Road*, by Louise Spiegler, Serena struggles against the dominant culture and her own tribal rules on a quest to control her future. She shares much of the journey with a young man, Shem, who is on his own quest. Both are rebelling against the expectations of their tribes, but in different ways and with different goals. While helping — and sometimes using — each other, they develop a complex relationship. Shem's story enhances Spiegler's exploration of choice.

Spiegler explains, "The dynamics that occur between Serena and Shem allow the story to be multi-layered: not only an outward quest — through inhospitable territory and with difficult challenges — but also an inner journey, in which Serena's knowledge of her own heart and her own identity unfolds."

Use Secondary Characters

In the Haunted books, supporting characters include the kids' mother, stepfather, and the young production assistant who's supposed to keep an eye on them. These characters sometimes pop up at inconvenient times, causing trouble. But when expanding book 1, I realized I could use my secondary characters more.

In the short version, I had their mother offer to spend the next day with them, pressuring them to solve the ghost's problem the first day. For the expanded version, I included another day in the timeline — and Mom did spend it with them. They had to conduct their secret investigations with Mom looking over their shoulders, which added both tension and humor. Supporting characters don't have to be mean or want to cause harm — they might just have different goals.

Tip: Look at your supporting characters one at a time. Could you use them more? How could they add more trouble for your main character? Could adding additional minor characters make the plot more complex?

Example: In *Freefall*, by Anna Levine, Aggie is eighteen and about to be drafted into the Israeli army. She goes to boot camp to see if she has the strength, both internal and physical, to cope with the challenges. She trains with a group of girls and ends up befriending one of them. Their friendship, which introduces a subplot and a seemingly minor character, later becomes crucial in forwarding the plot as Aggie has to take risks for this friendship.

Levine says that though she did not plan on Lily taking a major role in the novel, Lily became the perfect foil for Aggie. "Sometimes you need to let the characters lead you and you may discover ways of expanding upon the novel by exploring minor characters," Levine says.

Use Setting

In my first version of *The Ghost on the Stairs*, the kids watched some of the filming, but I didn't use the TV show much. I added one chapter where they try out the ghost hunter gadgets and another where their stepfather interviews people who have claimed to see the ghost. Both these offered opportunities for humor, as only the kids knew whether the gadgets were really working and whether the interview subjects were telling the truth. As an added bonus, one of the interview subjects turned into a major player in the first three books — a fake psychic who figures out Tania's gift and tries to exploit it.

Tip: Look for ways to use your setting to add complications. What if the weather changed? What if they went somewhere without cell phone reception? What if they had to pass through a bad neighborhood — or sneak through a rich gated community with a guard? If your setting could be Anywhere, USA, charge it up for dramatic value.

Example: Look at the movie *Sweet Home Alabama*. Would it be the same if the main character only had to go home to New Jersey?

I'm convinced that my changes made *The Ghost on the Stairs* stronger and more exciting, because I added more meat, not just fat and gristle. The techniques I learned also helped me develop the other books in the Haunted series. Try these tips if you're having trouble making your manuscript long enough. Even if you don't need to target a specific length, these tips can help you pack more meat into your manuscript.

Chris Eboch's Haunted series includes *The Ghost on the Stairs*, *The Riverboat Phantom* and *The Knight in the Shadows*. *The Ghost Miner's Treasure* is due out in 2012. Read the first chapters at www.chriseboch.com.

The Hollywood Touch

by Chris Eboch, first published in *Writer's Digest*

Authors dream of having their books made into movies. But even if your story never hits the big screen, you can make your work better by thinking like a scriptwriter. Apply these screenwriting tricks to writing your novel and breathe new life into your work.

Open Big

I missed the connection between screenplays and novels for a long time. But when a middle grade novel just wasn't connecting with readers, I consulted with my brother, Doug Eboch, who wrote the original screenplay for the film *Sweet Home Alabama*. After reading my manuscript, he told me, "You need a big opening scene. Think of visuals, color and movement — maybe a big party."

He has a good point: Begin your novel with action, not background, to grab the reader's attention. "Start with something big and memorable," says David Steinberg, who wrote the screenplay for *Slackers* and co-wrote *American Pie 2*. "And big isn't as important as memorable. It doesn't have to be a big explosion, but start off with something exciting, different, weird — something that makes the reader want to keep going."

Don Hewitt, who co-wrote the English-language screenplay for the Japanese animated film *Spirited Away,* agrees. But, he warns, don't just make up any big scene for the sake of drama. "Start with an event that affects the character," he says. Ideally, this event is a moment of change, where the character starts on a new path.

Establishing the protagonist's role in the story is one of the most important functions of an opening, whether in films or novels. Let the reader know the character's goals. "What does he want? What does he really need?" asks Steinberg. "What's his external goal? And what's his internal goal — what's this person's flaw, and how is he going to be a better person by the end?"

In addition, Doug says, "An opening scene should establish the genre. For comedy, I try to make a really funny opening." In one of his screenplays, *Quiver*, a woman finds Cupid's bow and arrow. "I open with Cupid to establish that it's a comedy with a supernatural element."

If the opening is exciting, funny, sad, or scary, the audience expects the entire movie — or book — to be the same. If the opening is boring, the reader assumes the rest is, too. I took my brother's advice. Now my first chapter has exotic scenery, magic, humor and a huge food fight. And I found a way to work important setup information into all that action.

Scene by Scene

Set high expectations, then satisfy them. Consider each scene in your novel. How can you make it bigger, more dramatic?

"Imagine the worst thing that could happen," Hewitt suggests, "and force the issue."

Doug stresses the effectiveness of "set pieces — the big, funny moment in a comedy, the big action scene in an action movie. The 'wow' moments that audiences remember later. Novelists can give readers those scenes they'll remember when they put the book down."

Yet even in big scenes, you must balance action and dialogue. Any long conversation where nothing happens is going to be boring. Steinberg says, "Movies are about people doing things, not about people talking about doing things." Even in comedies, he says, dialogue must be relevant to the plot. "Dialogue is funny because of the situation, not because it's inherently funny." The same goes for novels, too.

Long action scenes can be equally dull. "When you look at the page, it shouldn't be blocky with action," says Paul Guay, who co-wrote screenplays for *Liar, Liar, The Little Rascals* and *Heartbreakers.*

Adds Hewitt: "Try to be as economical as you can with the action, and as precise as you can. Break it up with specific dialogue to strengthen it."

Get to the Point

Above all, screenwriters know the value of editing — and so should you. Studios expect scripts to be within a certain length, generally 90 to 120 pages. Although some movies today run longer than that, any writer who turns in a 300-page script looks like an amateur. Novelists don't always have such stringent requirements, but there's still a valuable lesson here.

"You should always be moving on to the next story point," Guay says, "so you have almost no time to indulge in character flourishes or slow moments. If something is off-topic it has to go. Screenwriting teaches you to be ruthless."

Doug says, "I'll go back through every line and look for lazy writing, dialogue or description that doesn't advance the character or plot, and see if there's a better way to do that."

As for description, keep it short. "A little detail is good in the beginning," Steinberg claims, "but readers don't care what things look like on Page 3, let alone on Page 50. Use description sparingly, and only if it's really relevant."

Novelists who focus on action over description are a step closer to making their books page-turners. However, you must remember that you don't have the luxury of visual aids, as screenwriters do. Make up for the lack of visuals by appealing to all five senses. Just keep the story moving, and use short descriptions to advance the plot, not distract from it.

Finis

Novelists have some advantages over screenwriters. Hewitt says, "You're so sparse when writing a screenplay, but a novel's fun because you're able to explain the emotions more clearly, and you can use any voice. You have the freedom that you don't have in a screenplay."

Take advantage of that freedom in your manuscripts. But also consider what you can learn from the movie world. Open big, increase the drama in each scene, balance action and dialogue with just enough description to set the scene, and edit ruthlessly. The resulting story will be stronger and provide imagery on par with the visuals modern audiences are used to seeing in movies. Who knows? It may even increase the chances of your book being made into a movie.

On the Edge of Your Seat: Creating Suspense

by Sophie Masson

Suspense is what keeps a reader reading — wanting to know what happens. The suspense can be of all kinds, from wanting to know who the baddie is in a thriller to wanting to know whether the heroine is going to choose Mr. A or Mr. B as her love interest, to — well, just about anything, really! Creating and maintaining suspense is important in any kind of story or novel; it is especially so in the kinds of genres that are built around suspense: mysteries, thrillers, spy stories, fantasy. Here are some of my tips, honed over years of writing in many of those genres!

First of all, to create suspense you need:

Some background information.

But incomplete knowledge.

That is, from the beginning the author needs to already have something set up — to let the reader know something about a character and their situation, or the suspense won't happen — you have to care what happens for suspense to occur in the reader's mind.

You can build towards that or start immediately with a suspenseful mysterious beginning, but there must not be too many clues as to what might happen or the suspense will fizzle out before it's had a chance to happen. You need instead to build up the tension carefully, making the reader think that something is one way when it's another. But at the same time you can't play dirty tricks on them — you shouldn't for instance at the climax suddenly produce a character that wasn't there before — either in person or mentioned — as the villain, or the reader has a right to feel ripped off.

In my detective novel *The Case of the Diamond Shadow*, for instance, the true villain is hidden behind a smokescreen of red herrings — but is there all along. It's just that nobody even thinks of them in connection with the crime!

Character is very important in suspense. I think that plot itself, the driving machine of a story, is really at heart the unfolding of interaction between characters, good and bad. That is what creates situations and fuels tension. So you need to feel strongly for your characters especially the one or ones from whose point of view the action is viewed from, but also the others with whom they interact. If the characters feel real to your readers, then they will see when someone is acting out of character — and that will immediately set up suspense. Or say your main character trusts someone — really trusts them — and little by little they begin to change their minds, to suspect they're up to no good — excellent suspense too.

Very important is to *show* not *tell*. Building up a tense situation, the suspense, you need to not say "so and so was scared" but show it by characters' physical reactions: heart pounding; skin feeling cold; hair rising on your arms or back of neck; feeling blank; disbelief; time slowing down; all that in different degrees depending on whether it's fear or excitement or whatever. You the writer need to feel as though it is YOU experiencing it. You need to feel as though you're writing to find out what happens, just as a reader reads to find out what happens. You've got to be there with your character experiencing the thing every step of the way.

Using the first person narrative is a great way of dropping a reader right into a story and makes suspense easier to create. You can even do that with two split first-person points of view. For example, in my recent historical mystery novel, *The Understudy's Revenge*, the heroine Millie is knocked out, and her best friend Seth takes over the narration, also in first person. That increases the suspense, as Seth didn't know what had happened to Millie. The intertwining narratives made things even more exciting! But third person can work well, too. I've read — and written! — books which give you alternating points of view, not only from the hero or a friend, but also from a villain. It can work really well, if you're careful, but it's easy to lose suspense by doing that, too. Your reader should ideally be in the same position as your main character.

One good way of carrying suspense is to switch tenses. Start off in the past tense and then when the extraordinary or bad stuff is happening, switch to the present. Time really does seem to move differently when you're scared or excited or on tenterhooks — sentences and thoughts get shorter, choppier, and that creates a gripping feeling of suspense.

You can even create suspense in stories based on historical events, where readers already know what happened. I did that in my recent novel, *The Hunt for Ned Kelly*, which is set around the last year of the famous 19th century Australian outlaw Ned Kelly's life. The story's told in the form of the diary of 12 year old Jamie Ross and in one section he is writing about the siege at Glenrowan in Victoria, where Kelly made his last stand.

Now, I could have had him there watching, but I thought that was silly as it's well documented who was there and wasn't. I still wanted the suspense of the whole thing unfolding. What I did was have Jamie working for a newspaper as a messenger boy. The news is coming down the wire and they are printing heaps of updated editions and he's run off his feet trying to deliver them. People stop him in the street and ask him what's going on and he gabbles the story as it's come down the wires. It feels very immediate. A lot of readers have commented on how exciting they found it and how even though they knew what happened to Kelly, still they were taken up in the story so they felt anything could have happened!

But no matter what genre or medium you're writing in, you mustn't forget above all is to have a good payoff. It is no use building up excellent suspense, really ratcheting up the pressure till you think you're going to get this amazing revelation, and then it all goes limp because the truth behind it all is underwhelming. I read a book like that recently. It was a really excellent thriller, frightening, intriguing, scary, the suspense was killing me — and then, bang! A really silly motive is uncovered as the reason for the whole thing and it all fell flat on its face.

I really hate it as a reader when that happens, and so as a writer I try very hard to avoid it. That means I should have some idea of where my story is heading; that I know at least in outline what the ending is going to be, and what the motive behind the happenings is. I don't have to know everything, in fact I shouldn't — I want to be surprised as a writer, too, and to have adventures along the way — but I do want to create the best and most satisfying payoff.

Sophie Masson has published more than 50 novels internationally since 1990, mainly for children and young adults. A bilingual French and English speaker, raised mostly in Australia, she has a master's degree in French and English literature. Her most recent novel to be published in the USA, *The Madman of Venice* (Random House), was written for middle school children, grades ~6-10 and her recent historical novel, *The Hunt for Ned Kelly* (Scholastic Australia) won the prestigious Patricia Wrightson Prize for Children's Literature in the 2011 NSW Premier's Literary Awards. www.sophiemasson.org

The Promise of the First Chapter

by Chris Eboch, first published on the Institute of Children's Literature Rx for Writers website.

You'll hear it over and over again — opening lines are important. Your opening makes a promise about the rest of the story, article, or book. It tells readers what to expect, setting the stage for the rest of the story to unfold — and hopefully hooking their interest.

What You Promise

The first scene should identify your story's genre. This can be trickier than it sounds. Say it's a romance, but the main character doesn't meet the love interest until later. Can you at least suggest her loneliness or desire for romance? (And get that love interest in there as soon as possible!)

Maybe you're writing a story involving magic, time travel, ghosts, or a step into another dimension, but you want to show the normal world before you shift into fantasy. That's fine, but if we start reading about a realistic modern setting and then halfway through magic comes out of nowhere, you'll surprise your reader — and not in a good way. Your story will feel like two different stories clumsily stitched together.

If you're going to start "normal" and later introduce an element like magic or aliens, hint at what's to come. Maybe the main character is wishing that magic existed — that's enough to prepare the reader. In my novel *The Ghost on the Stairs*, we don't find out that the narrator's sister has seen a ghost until the end of chapter 2. But on the opening page, she comments that the hotel "looks haunted" and is "spooky." Those words suggest that a ghost story may be coming. That's enough to prep the reader. (The title doesn't hurt either.)

Your opening should also identify the story's setting. This includes when and where we are, if it's historical or set in another country or world. Once again, you don't want your reader to assume a modern story and then discover halfway through that it's actually a historical setting. They'll blame you for their confusion. In a contemporary story, you may not identify a specific city, but the reader should have a feel for whether this is inner-city, small-town, suburban, or whatever.

Who and What's Up

Your opening pages should focus on your main character. You may find exceptions to this rule, but your readers will assume that whoever is prominent in the opening pages is the main character. Switching can cause confusion. You should also establish your point of view early. If you'll be switching points of view, don't wait too long to make the first switch. In novels, typically you want to show your alternate point of view in the second chapter and then switch back and forth with some kind of regular rhythm.

And of course, you want some kind of challenge or conflict in your opening. This doesn't have to be the main plot problem — you may need additional set up before your main character takes on that challenge or even knows about it. But try to make sure that your opening problem relates to the main problem. It may even lead to it.

In *The Ghost on the Stairs*, Tania faints at the end of chapter 1. Jon does not yet know why, but this opening problem leads to the main problem — she'd seen a ghost. If I'd used an entirely different opening problem, say stress with their new stepfather, that would have suggested a family drama, not a paranormal adventure.

In a short story, you need to introduce your main conflict even more quickly. A story I sold to *Highlights* started like this:

> *Jaguar Paw watched the older Mayan boys play pok-a-tok. The ball skidded around the court as the players tried to keep it from touching the ground. They used their arms, knees, and hips, but never their hands or feet. The best pok-a-tok players were everybody's heroes. These boys were just practicing. But that meant Jaguar Paw could watch from the edge of the court.*

That opening paragraph, 64 words, introduces the main character, identifies the foreign, historical setting, includes a specific location (the ball court), and hints at Jaguar Paw's desire to be a ballplayer. Genre, setting, main character, and conflict, all up front.

The Fast Start

An opening introduces many elements of the story. Yet you can't take too long to set the scene, or your readers may lose interest. You want to start in a moment of action, where something is changing, and cut the background. But don't rush things — take a little time to set up the situation, so it makes sense and we care about the characters and what's happening to them.

Fast, but not too fast. How do you find the balance?

You can test your opening by seeing how much you can cut. What if you delete the first sentence, the first paragraph, the first page? Does the story still make sense? Does it get off to a faster start? For a novel, what if you cut the whole first chapter, or several chapters? If you can't cut, can you condense?

On the other hand, if your beginning feels confusing or rushed, you might want to try starting earlier in the story. Try setting up a small problem that grabs the reader's attention, luring them in until you can get to the main problem. In my novel *The Well of Sacrifice*, the Maya are dealing with famine, disease, and marauders in the early chapters, even before the king dies and an evil high priest tries to take over. That gives readers time to understand these characters and their unusual world.

My Egyptian mystery, *The Eyes of Pharaoh*, opens with the main character running — an active scene, even though she's merely running for pleasure. In the rest of that first chapter, Seshta, a young temple dancer, is focused on a dance contest she wants to win. This introduces a challenge and a goal, and the contest is a major subplot throughout the book, though not the primary plot line. By the end of the first chapter, Seshta's friend Reya, a young soldier, warns her that Egypt may be in danger. She doesn't believe him, but the reader has seen the seeds of the main plot, which will develop when Reya disappears and Seshta searches for him, uncovering a plot against the Pharaoh.

The inciting incident — the problem that gets the story going — should happen as soon as possible, but not until the moment is ripe. The reader must have enough understanding of the character and situation to make the incident meaningful. Too soon, and the reader is confused. Too late, and the reader gets bored first.

Options for Fast Starts:

- Start in the action, at a moment of change. Then work in the back story.

- Start with two people on the page.

- Start in the middle of a fight or other conflict.

- Start with a cliffhanger — something powerful about to happen.

- Start with a small problem that leads to the big problem, or is an example of the main problem.

Keeping Your Tone

With all the pressure to write a great opening, people often struggle to find an opening scene that is dramatic, powerful, and eye-catching! Something that will make the reader want to keep reading!!!

We may see our opening as something almost separate from the full manuscript — something we can submit to a first pages critique or send to an editor or agent who only wants to see a few pages as a sample. But treating the opening paragraphs as an ad may not be best for the rest of the manuscript. A clever, funny hook is great — but only if the rest of the book is also clever and funny.

Many readers will browse a book's opening pages in a library or bookstore to decide if they want to take the book home. If you offer the reader a fast-paced, action-packed opening, when your book is really a subtle emotional drama with lyrical descriptive writing, you're going to disappoint the readers who enjoyed the opening. Even worse, readers who would have enjoyed the whole book might never get past the opening page.

The same holds true for stories on a smaller scale. Even if your story only lasts a few pages, your readers are making judgments during your opening lines. Don't confuse them by starting one way and then turning the story into something else.

Opening Exercises

Try these exercises to explore how openings make promises.

Pick up one of your favorite novels. Reread the first chapter. What promises does it make? From your knowledge of the book, does it fulfill those promises? Repeat this exercise with other books. Try it with short stories and articles, judging the promises made in the first few lines.

When you start reading a new novel, pause at the end of the first chapter. Could you identify the genre, main character, point of view, and setting? Is the main character facing a challenge? Make a note of these promises. At the end of the book, decide whether each promise was fulfilled. Try reading short stories and articles this way as well.

Think about your work in progress. What do you want to promise? Check your first chapter for each of the following:

- Does it clearly identify the genre?

- Does it identify the setting, including time period, country, and urban/rural/suburban lifestyle? Does it suggest whether this is a school story, a family story, an epic interstellar journey, or whatever?

- Does it introduce the main character and possibly one or more other important characters?

- Does it clearly establish the point of view and the tone of the book (funny, lyrical, intellectual, or whatever)?

- Is a problem introduced quickly? If it is not the primary plot problem, does the opening challenge at least relate to or lead to the main problem?

Few authors wind up using their original openings. Some authors write a novel, then throw away the first chapter and write a new first chapter — the one that belongs there. It seems like it's almost impossible to write a strong opening until you've finished the rest of the book. The final version of the opening may actually be the last thing we write!

Openings are a struggle for many of us, but don't worry about the beginning during the first draft. Chances are it will change completely anyway, so wait until you have a solid plot before you start fine-tuning your opening. You need to know the rest of your story in order to figure out what your opening should be.

Don't stress about the opening during your early drafts, but do make sure you fix it later. Keep in mind that fixing the beginning may involve throwing it out altogether and replacing it with something else or simply starting later in the story. In the end, you'll have the beginning you need.

Hook 'Em Fast

by Lois Winston

As both a published author and a literary agent, I can clue you in on a dirty little secret: most editors and agents will toss a manuscript aside after a page or two if the voice/style/plot hasn't hooked them by that point.

I would like to distill this down further and suggest that an author needs to hook her readers with the opening sentence of her book. As someone who has read countless submissions, I've come across thousands of openings with what I can only describe as blah first sentences. The authors go on to compound the problem by adding several paragraphs, if not pages, of back-story and/or boring description. An author may have a fantastic story, but if she puts her readers to sleep before they get to that story, she's got a huge problem.

The first sentence of a book should make the reader want to read the second sentence. The hook doesn't have to be defined in the first sentence, but that first sentence should lead you into the next, and that one to the next, until you have a paragraph that becomes a hook that grabs the reader and won't let go. That first paragraph should do for the first page what the first sentence does for the first paragraph, and the first page should do for the subsequent pages what the first paragraph does for the first page.

Here's an example of a poorly written opening paragraph:

> My name is Anastasia Pollack. I'm a forty-two year old, pear-shaped, more than slightly overweight brunette crafts editor at American Woman magazine. A week ago I was living a typical middleclass life. I had a loving husband, two great sons, a job I looked forward to going to each morning, and a yellow rancher with white trim and a picket fence in a New Jersey suburb known for its good schools and easy commute into Manhattan. All that changed when my husband, who used to answer to tall, dark, and handsome but had turned into bald, paunchy, and boring over the years, dropped dead at a roulette table in Las Vegas when

he was supposed to be at a sales meeting in Harrisburg, Pennsylvania. That's when I learned of his secret gambling addiction and that he'd squandered away our life savings and left me up to my eyeballs in debt with a long line of bill collectors having my telephone number on speed dial. As if that wasn't bad enough, his loan shark is now demanding I pay back the fifty thousand dollars my husband borrowed from him. I don't have fifty thousand dollars. And last but not least, I'm stuck with my husband's mother, a card-carrying communist, living with me and my sons.

Now, here's the opening paragraph as it actually appeared in the published book:

I hate whiners. Always have. So I was doing my damnedest not to become one in spite of the lollapalooza of a quadruple whammy that had broadsided me last week. Not an easy task, given that one of those lollapalooza whammies had barged into my bedroom and was presently hammering her cane against my bathroom door. — Assault With a Deadly Glue Gun, by Lois Winston

The opening of a book should be filled with interesting action and/or dialogue that intrigues the reader and makes her want to continue reading. The opening of a book is meant to suck the reader into the world the author has created. Back-story can come later, trickling in to tease the reader to continue reading more, not as information dumps that pull the reader from the story. A good opening will include only the barest minimum of back-story that is essential for that moment.

As for description, it should be woven into the narrative and dialogue and limited to only that which is important to the scene at the moment the scene is taking place. Nothing bores a reader more than long paragraphs describing everything from the length of a heroine's hair to the color of her toenail polish. It pulls the reader from the story. And pulling the reader from the story is a bad thing. It adversely affects the pacing of the book, and good pacing is imperative in a well-written story.

Sometimes the plot and conflict might not be evident in the opening of a book, but there should be enough of a tease within that opening to give the reader an indication of events to come. In the example I gave above, the reader knows something is going to happen when the bathroom door is opened. This foreshadowing of something to come was accomplished without the long paragraph of back-story and description within the poorly written example.

If you want your readers to get lost in your plot, make sure you grab them with a dynamic opening.

Award-winning author **Lois Winston** writes the Anastasia Pollack Crafting Mysteries featuring magazine crafts editor and reluctant amateur sleuth Anastasia Pollack. *Assault With a Deadly Glue Gun*, the first book in the series, was a January 2011 release and received starred reviews from both *Publishers Weekly* and *Booklist. Kirkus Reviews* dubbed it, "North Jersey's more mature answer to Stephanie Plum." Lois is an award-winning crafts and needlework designer and an agent with the Ashley Grayson Literary Agency. www.loiswinston.com

How to Write Vivid Scenes

by Chris Eboch

In fiction writing, a scene is a single incident or event. However, a summary of the event is not a scene. Scenes are written out in detail, shown, not told, so we see, hear, and feel the action. They often have dialog, thoughts, feelings, and sensory description, as well as action.

A scene ends when that sequence of events is over. A story or novel is, almost always, built of multiple linked scenes. Usually the next scene jumps to a new time or place, and it may change the viewpoint character.

Think in terms of a play: The curtain rises on people in a specific situation. The action unfolds as characters move and speak. The curtain falls, usually at a dramatic moment. Repeat as necessary until you've told the whole story.

So how do you write a scene?

1. Place a character — usually your main character — in the scene.

2. Give that character a problem.

3. Add other characters to the scene as needed to create drama.

4. Start when the action starts — don't warm up on the reader's time.

5. What does your main character think, say, and do?

6. What do the other characters do or say?

7. How does your main character react?

8. What happens next? Repeat the sequence of actions and reactions, escalating tension.

9. Built to a dramatic climax.

10. End the scene, ideally with conflict remaining. Give the reader some sense of what might happen next — the character's next goal or challenge — to drive the plot forward toward the next scene. Don't ramble on after the dramatic ending, and don't end in the middle of nothing happening.

Scene endings may or may not coincide with chapter endings. Some authors like to use cliffhanger chapter endings in the middle of a scene and finish the scene at the start of the next chapter. They then use written transitions (*later that night, a few days later, when he had finished,* etc.) or an extra blank line to indicate a break between scenes within a chapter.

A scene can do several things, among them:

- Advance the plot.

- Advance subplots.

- Reveal characters (their personalities and/or their motives).

- Set the scene.

- Share important information.

- Explore the theme.

Ideally, a scene will do multiple things. It may not be able to do everything listed above, but it should do two or three of those things, if possible. It should always, always, advance the plot. Try to avoid having any scene that *only* reveals character, sets the scene, or explores the theme, unless it's a very short scene, less than a page. Find a way to do those things while also advancing the plot.

A scene often includes a range of emotions as a character works towards a goal, suffers setbacks, and ultimately succeeds or fails. But some scenes may have one mood predominate. In that case, try to follow with a scene that has a different mood. Follow an action scene with a romantic interlude, a happy scene with a sad or frightening one, a tense scene with a more relaxed one, to give the reader a break from one strong emotion.

Don't rush through a scene — use more description in scenes with the most drama, to increase tension by making the reader wait a bit to find out what happens. Important and dramatic events should be written out in detail, but occasionally you may want to briefly summarize in order to move the story forward. For example, if we already know what happened, we don't need to hear one character telling another what happened. Avoid that repetition by simply telling us that character A explained the situation to character B.

Avoid scenes that repeat previous scenes, showing another example of the same action or information. Your readers are smart enough to get things without being hit over the head with multiple examples. If you show one scene of a drunk threatening his wife, and you do it well, we'll get it. We don't need to see five examples of the same thing. Focus on writing one fantastic scene and trust your reader to understand the characters and their relationship. For every scene, ask: Is this vital for my plot or characters? How does it advance plot and reveal character? If I cut the scene, would I lose anything?

Connecting Scenes

Each scene is a mini-story, with its own climax. Each scene should lead to the next and drive the story forward, so all scenes connect and ultimately drive toward the final story climax.

A work of fiction has one big story question — essentially, will this main character achieve his or her goal? For example, in my children's historical fiction novel *The Eyes of Pharaoh*, the main character hunts for her missing friend. The story question is, "Will Seshta find Reya?" In *The Well of Sacrifice*, the story question is, "Will Eveningstar be able to save her city and herself from the evil high priest?"

In *Rattled* (written as Kris Bock), the big story question is, "Will Erin find the treasure before the bad guys do?" There may also be secondary questions, such as, "Will Erin find love with the sexy helicopter pilot?" but one main question drives the plot.

Throughout the work of fiction, the main character works toward that story goal during a series of scenes, each of which has a shorter-term scene goal. For example, in Erin's attempt to find the treasure, she and her best friend Camie must get out to the desert without the bad guys following; they must find a petroglyph map; and they must locate the cave.

You should be able to express each scene goal as a clear, specific question, such as, "Will Erin and Camie get out of town without being followed?" If you can't figure out your main character's goal in a scene, you may have an unnecessary scene or a character who is behaving in an unnatural way.

Yes, No, Maybe

Scene questions can be answered in four ways: Yes, No, Yes but..., and No and furthermore....

If the answer is "Yes," then the character has achieved his or her scene goal and you have a happy character. That's fine if we already know that the character has more challenges ahead, but you should still end the chapter with the character looking toward the next goal, to maintain tension and reader interest. Truly happy scene endings usually don't have much conflict, so save that for the last scene.

If the answer to the scene question is "No," then the character has to try something else to achieve that goal. That provides conflict, but it's essentially the same conflict you already had. Too many examples of the character trying and failing to achieve the same goal, with no change, will get dull.

An answer of "Yes, but…" provides a twist to increase tension. Maybe a character can get what she wants, but with strings attached. This forces the character to choose between two things important to her or to make a moral choice, a great source of conflict. Or maybe she achieves her goal but it turns out to make things worse or add new complications.

For example, in *Rattled*, the bad guys show up in the desert while Erin and Camie are looking for the lost treasure cave. The scene question becomes, "Will Erin escape?" This is answered with, "Yes, but they've captured Camie," which leads to a new set of problems.

"No, and furthermore…" is another strong option because it adds additional hurdles — time is running out or your character has a new obstacle. It makes the situation worse, which creates even greater conflict. In my current work in progress, tentatively titled *Whispers in the Dark* (written as Kris Bock), one scene question is, "Will Kylie be able to notify the police in time to stop the criminals from escaping?" When this is answered with, "No, and furthermore they come back and capture her," the stakes are increased dramatically.

One way or another, the scene should end with a clear answer to the original question. Ideally that answer makes things worse. The next scene should open with a new specific scene goal (or occasionally the same one repeated) and probably a review of the main story goal. Here's an example from *The Eyes of Pharaoh*:

Scene question: "Will Seshta find Reya at the army barracks?"

Answer: "No, and furthermore, she thinks the general lied to her, so Reya may be in danger."

Next scene: "Can Seshta spy on the general to find out the truth, which may lead her to Reya?"

Over the course of a novel, each end-of-scene failure should get the main character into worse trouble, leading to a dramatic final struggle.

Cause and Effect

One of the ironies of writing fiction is that fiction has to be more realistic than real life. In real life, things often seem to happen for no reason. In fiction, that comes across as unbelievable. We expect stories to follow a logical pattern, where a clear action causes a reasonable reaction. In other words, cause and effect.

The late Jack M. Bickham explored this pattern in *Scene & Structure*, from Writer's Digest Books. He noted that every cause should have an effect, and vice versa. This goes beyond the major plot action and includes a character's internal reaction. When action is followed by action with no internal reaction, we don't understand the character's motives. At best, the action starts to feel flat and unimportant, because we are simply watching a character go through the motions without emotion. At worst, the character's actions are unbelievable or confusing.

In *Manuscript Makeover* (Perigee Books), Elizabeth Lyon suggests using this pattern: stimulus — reaction/emotion — thoughts — action.

- Something happens to your main character (the stimulus);

- You show his emotional reaction, perhaps through dialog, an exclamation, gesture, expression, or physical sensation;

- He thinks about the situation and makes a decision on what to do next;

- Finally, he acts on that decision.

This lets us see clearly how and why a character is reacting. The sequence may take one sentence or several pages, so long as we see the character's emotional and intellectual reaction, leading to a decision.

Bickham offered these suggestions for building strong scenes showing proper cause and effect:

The stimulus must be external — something that affects one of the five senses, such as action or dialog that could be seen or heard.

The response should also be partly external. In other words, after the character's emotional response, she should say or do something. (Even deciding to say nothing leads to a reaction we can see, as the character turns away or stares at the stimulus or whatever.)

The response should immediately follow the stimulus. Wait too long and the reader will lose track of the original stimulus, or else wonder why the character waited five minutes before reacting.

Be sure you word things in the proper order. If you show the reaction before the action, it's confusing: "Lisa hurried toward the door, hearing pounding." For a second or two, we don't know why she's hurrying toward the door. In fact, we get the impression that Lisa started for the door *before* she heard the pounding. Instead, place the stimulus first: "Pounding rattled the door. Lisa hurried toward it."

If the response is not obviously logical, explain it, usually with the responding character's feelings/thoughts placed between the stimulus and the response.

Here's an example where the response is not immediately logical:

> *Knocking rattled the door. (Stimulus)*
>
> *Lisa waited, staring at the door. (Action)*

Why is she waiting? Does she expect someone to walk in, even though they are knocking? Is she afraid? Is this not her house? To clarify, include the reaction:

> *Knocking rattled the door. (Stimulus)*
>
> *Lisa jumped. (Physical Reaction) It was after midnight and she wasn't expecting anyone. Maybe it was a mistake. Maybe they'd go away. (Thoughts)*
>
> *She waited, staring at the door. (Responsive Action)*

In some cases the response may be logical and obvious without including thoughts and emotions in between. For example, if character A throws a ball and character B raises a hand to catch it, we don't need to hear character B thinking, "There's a ball coming at me. I had better catch it." But don't assume your audience can always read between the lines. Often as authors *we* know why our characters behave the way they do, so we assume others will understand and we don't put the reaction and thoughts on the page. This can lead to confusion.

In one manuscript I critiqued, the character heard mysterious voices. I assumed they were ghosts, but the narrator never identified them that way. Did he think they were something else? Did he think he was going crazy? Had he not yet decided? I couldn't tell. The author may have assumed the cause of the voices was obvious, so she didn't need to explain the character's reaction. But it just left me wondering if I was missing something — or if the character was. Err on the side of showing your character's thoughts.

Link your scenes together with scene questions and make sure you're including all four parts of the scene — stimulus, reaction/emotion, thoughts, and action — and you'll have vivid, believable scenes building a dramatic story.

Hanging by the Fingernails: Cliffhangers

by Chris Eboch

Several years ago I had the opportunity to ghostwrite a novel about a well-known girl sleuth. (You would recognize her name.) I knew the series used cliffhanger chapter endings. That seemed easy enough — find a dramatic moment and end the chapter.

Turns out writing strong cliffhangers is a little trickier than that. The editor responded to my effort with this comment: "I would like to see more of a slow build-up toward the intense action. In horror movies, it's always the ominous music and the main character slowly opening the closet door that scares us the most, not the moment right after she opens the door."

She's noting the difference between *suspense* and *surprise*.

When something happens suddenly and unexpectedly, that's a surprise. For example, if you are walking down the street debating where to have lunch and something falls off a window ledge onto your head, you'll be surprised (assuming you're still conscious). But since the surprise came out of nowhere, it wasn't suspenseful.

When writing we may be tempted to keep secrets and then let them out — *bang!* But suspense comes from suspecting that something will happen and worrying about it or anticipating it.

To build up truly dramatic cliffhanger chapter endings, give the reader clues that something bad — or excitingly good — is going to happen. Here's an example from *Haunted: The Ghost on the Stairs*, a novel for ages 8 to 12. The narrator, Jon, isn't sure he believes his little sister Tania when she says she can see ghosts, but goes with her to look for one as their stepfather films his ghost hunter TV show.

> At the top of the stairs, my stepfather stood in the glare of a spotlight, a few feet away from a camera. I took a step backward and tugged at Tania's arm. No one had seen us yet, and we could still escape.
>
> Tania turned to me. The look in her eyes made my stomach flip.

The moment isn't bad for a cliffhanger chapter ending, but it could use some more buildup. Here's how the chapter ended in the published book:

> *At the top of the stairs, my stepfather stood in the glare of a spotlight, a few feet away from a camera. I took a step backward and tugged at Tania's arm. No one had seen us yet, and we could still escape.*
>
> *She didn't back up. She swayed.*
>
> *I took a quick step forward and put my arm around her so she wouldn't fall. I looked down into her face. I'd never seen anyone so white. White as death. Or white as a ghost.*
>
> *"Tania," I hissed. I gave her a shake. She took a quick breath and dragged her eyes away from the staircase and to my face. The look in them made my stomach flip.*

The first thing you may notice is that the revised version is longer. To get the most out of dramatic moments, you actually slow the pace by using more detail. Focus on using sensory details with an emotional impact.

Powerful Paragraphing

Description can usually be kept together in one longer paragraph. Action reads better when broken into short paragraphs. Short paragraphs can actually make the story read faster, because the eye moves more quickly down the page. You can also emphasize an important sentence by starting a new paragraph or even putting that sentence into a paragraph by itself. For example, consider the following two action scenes:

> Example 1:
>
> My car picked up speed as it rolled down the steep hill. The light at the bottom turned yellow so I stepped on the brakes. The car didn't slow down. The light turned red as I pressed harder, leaning back in my seat, using my whole leg to force the brake pedal toward the floor. I sped toward the intersection while other cars entered from the sides. I sailed into the intersection, horns blaring and brakes squealing around me as I passed within inches of two cars coming from each side.

Example 2:

> My car picked up speed as it rolled down the steep hill. The light at the bottom turned yellow.
> I stepped on the brakes. The car didn't slow down.
> The light turned red.
> I pressed harder, leaning back in my seat, using my whole leg to force the brake pedal toward the floor.
> My car sped toward the intersection. Other cars entered from the sides.
> I sailed into the intersection. Horns blared and brakes squealed around me.
> I passed within inches of two cars coming from each side.

These use nearly the same words. The only differences are that in the second version I broke up some long sentences into short ones, and I use seven paragraphs instead of one. I think the second version captures more of the breathless panic that the narrator would be feeling.

Don't Cheat

Because cliffhangers are a powerful tool to keep the reader turning the pages, you may be tempted to build that suspense even when nothing much happens afterward. You can get away with that kind of trick once in a while, especially if the result is intentionally humorous. For example, if a character thinks a wolf is stalking her, and it turns out to be a big friendly dog, you get the buildup of suspense followed by amusing relief.

But if you play tricks too often, your readers will learn to expect it and won't be worried the next time your character seems to be in danger. So use cliffhangers wisely. You get the reader worried at the end of one chapter. The payoff at the beginning of the next chapter is that something dramatic did happen.

Sometimes authors use "If I had known…" chapter endings. You know, "If she had known how that day would turn out, she never would have gotten out of bed." Personally, I don't like this technique. It takes me out of the story because we're suddenly jumping to a different time, when the character did have that knowledge, or else slipping into a heavy-handed authorial comment. It's like the author is saying, "I know it's not exciting now, but it will be!" I don't want promises, I want drama. Now.

Even when things are going well, you can end a chapter with foreboding. Here's an example from Haunted book 4, *The Ghost Miner's Treasure*, when everything seems under control:

> *I still had a bad feeling. I tried to shake it off. What did I think I was, psychic?*
> *But I didn't have to be psychic to know that nothing comes easily, or without a price.*

This lets the reader know that the characters have challenges ahead. Our experiences as readers have taught us to expect reversals, so you need only a hint of complications ahead to let the reader know something is going to go wrong.

Quiet Cliffhangers

If you don't have an action novel, you can still have dramatic chapter endings, whether or not the characters are in physical danger. In a young adult romance, for example, the drama may come from social humiliation at school and awkward or exciting moments with the love interest. Play up those moments for maximum effect.

Not every chapter has to end with a major cliffhanger. Sometimes it feels more natural to end the chapter at the end of the scene, especially if that scene is followed by a jump to a different time and place. You can end in a quieter moment, so long as you're still looking forward. Here's an example from *The Amethyst Road*, by Louise Spiegler. Serena has been searching for her mother for over 200 pages, believing that her mother will be able to put the family back together. But when she finds her, this happens:

> *Mother's smile vanished. "But, Serena, how can I help? The Cruelty won't even let me care for my own children." She raised her face to mine. "Look at me. I can hardly help myself, daughter. How can I help you?*

This works as a cliffhanger because the response is a challenge to Serena's expectations and hope. What will she do now? The reader will turn the page, wanting to know.

In this example from *The Farwalker's Quest*, by Joni Sensel, the two main characters have a quiet moment before setting out again on their journey:

> *They worked out a plan. After Pres left them to sleep, Ariel and Zeke only lay back and gazed at the ceiling. His toes, warm against her calf, seemed to say all that was needed between them. This night in a real bed would be the last for a long time to come.*

This quiet cliffhanger looks towards the future, reminding the reader that their troubles are not over.

Cliffhangers are a powerful tool to build suspense. Choose a dramatic moment, expand the moment with sensory details for drama, and use short paragraphs and sentences for impact.

You'll keep readers turning the page.

Message, Moral, Meaning: The Theme

by Chris Eboch

Most writers focus on characters, plot, or both as they write. Setting may play a small or large role. But one element is sometimes neglected: theme.

Writers shouldn't "preach" in their fiction, of course. Readers generally want an entertaining story, not a lecture. But every work of fiction does include a theme. (Really. I've led workshops where we try to come up with an example that doesn't, but if you think about it, everything seems to have some kind of theme. Even a simple haiku may have a theme about the beauty of nature, while a newspaper report might point out the dangers of our modern world.)

Yet many writers, even advanced ones, suffer from a thematic challenge: the theme may be unclear, perhaps even to the writer herself.

Author Holly Cupala says, "Throughout the writing of *Tell Me A Secret* (HarperCollins), I would hit on something and think, This is the theme! Then a little later, No, *this* is the theme. It seems to be an evolving — or perhaps devolving — process, getting to the heart of the story, layer by layer. I even found an old blog of mine where I thought I'd hit on the theme and had the same experience — the chills, the thunderous weight of the moment you realize, 'Wait, wait, wait. *This* is the theme.' I think on some level I've been right every time, chipping away at the complex layers of what it means to write something as truthfully as possible."

As this successful novelist shows, you don't always have to know your theme before you start. Sometimes you may discover your message as you write the story. Or you may start with one idea in mind and change it as you go. You may even realize that you don't quite believe your original theme — writing the story may help you explore new aspects of that idea, uncovering complexities and contradictions. This can result in a deeper, more meaningful story, so let that process unfold.

Uma Krishnaswami says, "I did not know the theme of *Naming Maya* (Farrar Straus Giroux) until I was through the fifth draft. I never thought of it as theme, even then, because words like 'theme' that come from literary criticism rather than craft tend to shut me down. Instead I spent a lot of time asking myself, 'What is this story really about? What does Maya long for?' She thinks she wants her father back but that wasn't the want that drove the book. I wrote myself fake jacket blurbs, trying to get at that elusive heart. By that time I was well into my sixth draft. The thematic through-line of identity emerged quite suddenly one day."

She adds, "Truthfully, I am not sure that we should be thinking too much, too soon, about theme. It's a fragile concept, and we need to allow it to come out of the subconscious mind, which is where the best writing takes place. In my opinion, when themes are planted in place too intentionally, stories come across as heavy-handed and with the author's stamp far too clearly imprinted."

Focusing too much on a specific theme at the beginning can result in stiff characters, a clunky plot, and that dreaded preachiness. But you should definitely know your theme before you finish your final draft. That way you can edit to make sure your story best supports your theme.

My World View

When trying to identify your theme, start big and then narrow your focus. Can you define your theme in one word? Is it about love, hope, courage, sacrifice? Once you've identified that word, try to state your theme as a single, clear sentence. What do you want to say about that word?

For example, if your novel is about sacrifice, what about it? Is your character making sacrifices for her own future, for a loved one, for her country, for an ideal? What does she have to sacrifice? Narrowing in on the specifics can help you pinpoint your theme.

Once you've clarified your theme, work backward. Does your novel truly support it? Maybe you've decided that your theme is "The greater good is more important than the individual's desire." In that case, your main character should be giving up a desire in order to help a larger group. But perhaps you liked your character so much that you ended with her helping the group and getting what she wanted as well. That weakens your message, and suggests a different theme, "Good will be rewarded." You might want to reconsider your ending.

Try to envision all the different messages someone could get from your story. I've read several unpublished children's stories about young animal characters who are ostracized because of some physical flaw. Then something happens that requires their particular abilities. These writers are trying to say that everyone has special qualities or that a perceived flaw can turn out to be a strength. Good message. But on the other hand, these stories could suggest that you won't be accepted unless you prove yourself through heroic action. That might encourage kids to look for ways to show off, rather than to accept themselves as they are.

Having readers miss your intended theme can become a big problem, if they are seeing messages that go against your beliefs. Find a few people to read your story — ideally people among your target audience — and ask them what message they take away. Make sure their response is in line with your ideals.

Don't expect your readers to pick out your theme exactly, however. If they do, you're probably not being subtle enough. Just make sure they find a valuable message. In my Mayan historical adventure, *The Well of Sacrifice*, I knew my main theme: make your own decisions and stand on your own. My heroine, Eveningstar, learns that she can't depend on her heroic older brother, her parents, the government, or religion to solve the city's problems. When they all fail her, she has to act by herself.

One young reader wrote me and said, "The book...helped me think to never give up, even in the worst of times, just like what happened to Eveningstar." I'm happy to inspire a reader to "never give up," even if that wasn't my main theme. And perhaps readers will be subtly influenced by my primary message, even if they don't recognize it while reading.

Too Many Messages?

For younger readers and short stories, you need to keep the theme simple. The longer the story or novel, and the older the reader, the more complex you can be. At first a book may appear to be a humorous romance, but as the story unfolds, it may reveal a theme about honesty in relationships.

Your theme doesn't have to be obvious from your first paragraph, and probably shouldn't be. In fact, the theme may only be clear from the final twist in the story. The theme can be revealed through what the main character learns, how she changes, what she gains or loses.

As part of your revisions (or in the planning stage, if you're really organized), work on your character in order to set up your theme. Use her virtues and vices. How will her strengths help her? What weaknesses does she have to overcome? Make sure these tie into the theme. If your character must learn about honesty, make sure that it will be possible but difficult for her. Maybe she craves intimacy but is afraid no one will like her if she shows her true self.

For longer works, think about how you can use other characters or subplots to support or expand on your theme. Maybe your main character learns to be honest in her relationships, and so develops a loving connection with her boyfriend. In contrast, her friend might keep lying in order to make a good impression, and get dumped or wind up with a shallow, dissatisfying relationship. A subplot with the main character's divorced parents could explore the theme in yet another way.

Although you should be able to clearly identify a single main theme, you may have additional themes. Holly Cupala says, "The theme I seem to be writing is that you can't find yourself in other people. It's very much there in *Tell Me A Secret* as well as *Don't Breathe a Word* (HarperTeen). Then there are the peripheral themes — looking to the past for meaning versus looking to the future for purpose, wanting to be loved for who you are, trading blame for hope."

Multiple themes can give a novel extra depth and power. However, don't let your story get cluttered with too many themes, especially wildly different ones. If you try to share everything you believe about life in one story, it will just feel cluttered and confusing. Focus on one primary theme, and save the others for different works.

Five Revision Passes (ok, seven maybe. . .)

by Suzanne Morgan Williams

Here is a snapshot of some of the techniques that work for me to revise and polish my manuscripts. These are ideas, not rules. I hope they spark some ideas for your novel.

1. Characters — Write down the name of every major character and then of every minor one. For each major character describe the character arc. In what chapters do the changes happen? Does this make sense? Do they all have some relationship to the protagonist? What is it? If two characters serve the same purpose, do you need them both?

2. Action — Go through your book and for *each chapter* write down exactly what happens. Don't include anything emotional. Just write down the action. Are there chapters where nothing physical happens? That are all talk or all reflection or where the only thing that happens is that someone comes over and unpacks their suitcase? Sometimes a chapter works with all reflection or all interaction between two characters but usually we want to see something happen in the physical world in each chapter. This will keep your book from being slow.

3. Setting — Check your manuscript for places where you can describe the place, the smells, the warmth of the sun or drip of fog. Use the environment to reflect the action. If you have a choice of places to have a scene (which you often do — kitchen, in a park, at a band practice, hiking on a mountain) be sure you choose a place that supports your intention. How many chase scenes have you seen through old falling down factories? Or through storm drains? They could chase the person through a park just as well. The setting ups the ante on the suspense. Some scenes have to be in a classroom or on a battlefield but others simply are establishing relationships or end with someone getting caught lying. These could be done in a number of spots in your world. Choose the places that echo your emotional intent.

4. Voice — Make sure your characters have their own voices. In first person your narrator and your main character will share a voice. Be sure it is relatively easy to read. Also your narrator will have to be the same age as your protagonist. In first person you may limit beautiful prose because your protagonist wouldn't talk that way. Read through the dialogue of major characters — maybe read it to a friend. Just read lines that one character speaks. Can they tell who it is? They should be able to. If they can't tell one character's distinctive voice from another's you need to change their language a bit.

It may not be so important that minor characters have distinctive voices but it doesn't hurt. And don't give anyone a voice that would be confused with your narrator. To fix it: Think about your character. How do people like him or her talk? Give him a favorite saying or exclamation. Make the rhythm of his speech a little different. Go to a café and eavesdrop. What kind of phrasing and slang do people use? Do the older people speak differently from the young ones? What words do kids actually use?

If you still can't hear the voices, take some time to interview your characters. Write out your questions first, then let them answer in their own words. Write their voices in first person, even if they are in third person in your book. Imagine you are hearing them answer the questions — not that you are them answering the questions — and write down what they say. Listen. This speech pattern should not necessarily be yours.

5. Rhythm/language/timing — Read your manuscript out loud. Fix any place that makes you stumble. Listen to the language. Decide in each section how fast the action should be moving. Short sentences speed up the action. Long ones with lots of phrases and descriptions slow it down. Imagine, would your protagonist have time to describe the cobblestones while he is running for his life? No, but you could get that in quickly with "he raced down the street, his steps beating loud on the cobblestones." There we get a sound, some fast action verbs, and we know there are stones. We don't need to know they are ancient or that they are brown and orange, or even that they are smooth, in a fast scene.

On the other hand, if the protagonist has just arrived in the city and is lost and looking around, she might take note of her surroundings "The grey cobblestones were uneven under my feet. I had to look down, balancing with each step. I stopped and looked closer. Each one was worn smooth in the center by how many feet? They were ancient." Match your language rhythm to your action.

6. Timing overall — Your entire manuscript should have an ebb and flow, a rise to the climax and an exhale at the end. The timing of the scenes and actions should vary to hold the readers' attention. Too much action is exhausting — save that for the end. Too much narration will put your reader to sleep. Long chunks of dialogue need to have a purpose. A normal chapter will have some action, some description, some dialogue, some interior thought.

To see how yours measures up, take markers of different colors and mark off each type of writing. Do you have a chapter that is all narration? Is there one that is all action? Is there a reason for this? In general, after you've marked a chapter you should see three or four colors. You will have chunks of chapters that are more action oriented, others that are more reflective, but they all need a little of several types of writing to work. Do you see a crescendo in action toward the end? Is there more description in the beginning as you set the scene? This is normal. Use this tool to help you consciously think about the rhythm of your story.

7. And finally — If you're writing for a young audience, is it kid friendly? For this reading get yourself in the mood. Remember what life was like when you were ten or sixteen or however old your reader will be. Go to a park or a mall and watch some kids if you need to. Reacquaint yourself with school curriculum — do third graders know about jet propulsion or will they need a little help understanding it? What about dinosaurs? Volcanoes?

Be sure you are thinking like a child. Now read through the story. What bores you? What don't you care about? What sounds really adult? When would you say, "Gosh, Mom, do you have to tell me that again?" Use this pass to add some real kid-isms. A prank, or an over-the-top reaction to a situation, or fear, or whatever your young protagonist might feel that escaped you on the other passes. And what about *language*? Be sure you aren't putting words in your kids' mouths that they just wouldn't say.

Suzanne Morgan Williams is the author of the middle grade novel *Bull Rider*, published by Margaret K. McElderry (Simon and Schuster). *Bull Rider* is a Junior Library Guild selection, Western Heritage Award Winner, and has been included on several state award lists. Besides working on fiction, Suzanne is author of several nonfiction books for children and young adults. Her newest nonfiction book is *China's Daughters*, from Pacific View Press. Suzanne is a frequent speaker at schools, libraries, writers' conferences, and teacher and librarian events. www.suzannemorganwilliams.com

More Advice from the Pros

I hope you found these essays educational and inspiring. To wrap things up, here are more words of wisdom on the subject of plotting, from professional writers working in a variety of genres.

Introducing Characters

by Dorothy Francis

From the start, introduce your characters — all of them, if possible, in the first 20 percent of your book. Impossible, you say. No, it's possible, if you plan carefully. You needn't have every character appear on scene during the book's beginning. However, you'll have a better chance of drawing your reader into your story and holding him there if you show off-scene characters by referring to them in dialogue, or just by hinting at their existence. This prepares the reader to meet your characters later, and this mini-introduction adds to the suspense of the tale.

Of course, there are exceptions to this rule. Sometimes if a plot starts to lag, you can revive it by introducing a character the reader hasn't met before. Use this technique when and if you need it.

Award-winning author **Dorothy Francis** writes short stories and novels, including the Key West mystery series. www.dorothyfrancis.com

The Unity of Character and Plot

by Andrea J. Wenger

Several years ago, at the North Carolina Writers Network conference, I attended a session where the instructor claimed that character *is* plot. While I understand her point, I think she went too far. Many things happen in our lives that we can't control. In fiction, the response to external events demonstrates character and propels plot. But generally, by the end of the story, the protagonist becomes proactive instead of responsive, and the protagonist's positive action creates the climax.

Character and plot must work in harmony. For the story to be believable, the actions the character takes must be consistent with the character you've created. For instance, imagine if two of Shakespeare's great tragic figures, Hamlet and Othello, were the protagonist in each other's stories. How would those plays go?

Act I, Scene 1: The ghost of the old king tells Othello to avenge the old king's death by killing Claudius.
Act I, Scene 2: Othello kills Claudius.
The End

No story, right? And if Iago hinted to Hamlet that Desdemona were cheating on him, Hamlet would answer, "You cannot play upon me."

For the two plays to work, *Othello*'s hero must be action-oriented, while *Hamlet*'s hero must be introspective.

Keep in mind, though, that when under extreme stress, people (and characters) behave in ways they never would otherwise. In *Writing the Breakout Novel*, Donald Maass advises novelists to imagine something their character would never think, say, or do — then create a situation where the character thinks, says, or does exactly that. If it's critical to your story that your character behave in uncharacteristic ways, put that character in an environment of increasing stress, until the point that the character's "shadow" takes over.

Isabel Myers, co-author of the Myers-Briggs Type Indicator, defined the shadow function as the least developed part of our personality. Even in the best of times, we may have difficulty using this function in a rational and mature manner. When someone is under stress, and the shadow takes charge, the results can be disastrous.

In your own stories, do character and plot work in harmony? If a character behaves in an uncharacteristic way, be sure to show that the character is under enough stress to make the action believable.

Andrea J. Wenger is professional writer specializing in technical, freelance, and creative writing. Her short fiction has appeared in *The Rambler*. She is currently working on a women's fiction novel. She blogs and speaks on the subject of writing and personality. She is a regular contributor to Carolina Communiqué, a publication of the Carolina Chapter of the Society for Technical Communication. www.WriteWithPersonality.com.

Thoughts On Plotting

by Mary Reed

Let us suppose you are about to begin work on your outline, a necessary evil when writing fiction and a penance for many authors, including myself.

You have some idea of the plotline and its twists and turns, your cast of characters, the clues and denouement. In the writing the plot will change (especially towards the end) and quite possibly new characters demand to be included — if they do, take notice! Now sit down and start writing.

Then look at your rough draft and put on your critical hat — ask yourself: does the plot follow logical lines? Do developments naturally build on what the characters knew up to the last chapter? Have you explained how they know (unless certain things must be concealed a little longer for plot purposes)?

Be careful nobody does anything based on something which at that particular point they could not possibly have known — when revising, this sort of error can easily occur, especially if you are moving chunks of text from one place to another.

Try to maintain a balance between stretches of text and conversation so that there are not long passages of one or the other. The old advice to "show, not tell" is as golden as ever.

For characters, avoid having their names beginning with the same letter unless it is important to the plot.

[For mysteries,] hide the clues in plain sight (for example, insert one into a list of what was in Lady Muckamuck's handbag or among the stuff found on the kitchen table at 94 Dogbone Alley, Limehouse, when the coppers burst in). This ensures you are fair with the reader, who then has a chance to solve the mystery before your protagonist — this, of course, assumes you are not writing the sort of book where the culprit is known from the first chapter and the protagonist's problem is catching them and foiling their evil designs.

Mary Reed co-authors the Lord Chamberlain historical mysteries and other tales of detection with her husband Eric Mayer. *Nine For The Devil*, the ninth novel in the Lord Chamberlain series, relates their protagonist's investigation into the death of Empress Theodora and will be published in March 2012 by Poisoned Pen Press. http://home.earthlink.net/~maywrite/

These thoughts first appeared in an interview conducted several years ago by Alan Bishop for his Criminal History website. www.criminal-history.co.uk/

Plotting Murder with Secrets and Surprises

by Jan Christensen

Here are some ideas you might want to think about when plotting your murder mystery:

- Give every character at least one secret.

- Give every character a good reason to NOT want to talk to your detective.

- The detective suspects everyone she talks to, and finds out if each person had motive, opportunity, and means. One out of two interviews she finds a clue and/or red herring — she may not know it's a clue when she notices it. Scatter them around. Use senses — see, hear, smell, taste, touch.

- Every character tells at least one lie when talking to the detective.

- Have the detective find two or more different suspects, at different times, in awkward positions — either overhearing something or seeing something which is suspect.

- Most every character the detective talks to has a reasonable motive for murdering the victim.

- Most every character had the opportunity to murder the victim, even if he gives an alibi.

- Most every character had the means to murder the victim.

- Several characters implicate another character, either overtly or subvertly. They give possible motive, opportunity, and/or means for other character. (Can implicate different characters.)

Extras:

- If the whole story doesn't take place in one different or exciting location, put in at least one unique setting — it can be as small as a house or pocket park or as big as an ocean.

- Use one character with a unique/interesting occupation or hobby. But tie it into the mystery somehow.

- When ideas come to you as you write, stick them in, even if you think they are out of place. You'd be surprised what your subconscious can come up with later to tie it together. And if that doesn't happen, you can easily delete it.

- Have someone who's not the bad guy totally opposed to the detective detecting. A romantic interest, a mother, a cop, aunt or uncle, for example.

And most important:

Have fun with your plot. Because if you do, your readers probably will as well.

Jan Christensen is an author of over 50 published short stories and a novel, *Sara's Search*, in which amateur sleuth Sara learns secrets, meets quirky characters and dashes between metropolitan NJ and NYC to solve her father's murder. www.janchristensen.com

Plotting with Scene Cards

by Mike Nettleton

Writing as a team is always an adventure. My wife Carolyn J. Rose and I have co-authored five books, four of them mysteries and one a young-adult fantasy, and have made great use of file cards to keep our plotting and character traits and tags straight.

With *The Big Grabowski* and its sequel we juggled sixteen point-of-view characters, each with their own story arc and role in solving the mystery of who offed the obnoxious and greedy land developer Vince Grabowski. By assigning each character a color-coded card, we could thumbnail scenes that featured them as we created setting, conflict, and scene goals.

Then we would start arranging the scene cards on a large flat surface and juggle them around as needed. At a glance we could see who hadn't shown up in a while and we could create additional scenes to feature them. Since Molly Donovan, ace reporter for the North Coast Flotsam, was our amateur sleuth and the only character in first person, her scenes needed to show up more often than the others. We've found that using the file cards kept us from going adrift and kept the pace hot and the story momentum flowing.

Mike Nettleton is co-author of *The Big Grabowski, Sometimes a Great Commotion* (sequel), *The Hard Karma Shuffle, The Crushed Velvet Miasma* (sequel), and *The Hermit of Humbug Mountain.* www.deadlyduomysteries.com/

Three Tips on Plotting

by Vijaya Bodach

1. When you write for young children, think of small problems — a lost toy, fear of a spider, or not getting your way. You can even have an incident story. For example, in my story "Six-Inch Squares" (*Ladybug*), a little boy cuts up squares from old clothes that no longer fit him. He doesn't cut off his finger, nor does he poke his sister's eye out. There's no drama. So what's the pay-off? A surprise: Mom makes him a birthday quilt.

2. If you like to write short stories, begin right before the climax, before the big burn, before all hell breaks loose. It makes for a fast-paced story.

3. I always ask, "Why?" Why would my character do this thing? It helps me to stay true to my character. I often come up with a neat plot twist, only to realize that it won't work because my character wouldn't do that. So, either I change my character, give him the motivation to do what I want him to do, or if it absolutely cannot happen, then the plot needs to change. This can be difficult when I plot a story carefully, but when I follow my characters organically through the space I create for them, they surprise me, becoming flesh-and-blood. Character and plot are inextricably linked.

Vijaya Bodach is a scientist-turned-children's writer who has published over 60 magazine pieces and over 30 science books for young readers. www.vijayabodach.com

Surprising Your Readers

by Deby Fredericks

I don't know about you, but I have some ornery first readers. They enjoy figuring things out before I reveal them. No matter how artful the red herrings and how obscure the clues, my husband and friends are constantly guessing the surprises.

Since I pride myself on creating original stories instead of rehashing best-sellers, this stings. Does it mean I should keep my day job because all my ideas are lame and predictable? On the contrary. I take it as a challenge.

If the first readers figure things out too quickly, that just means I need to bring more to the telling. Extra twists after the first one. Depth and meaning beyond the obvious. That way, even if they saw through my artifice, there was a reason for them to keep reading.

So my husband knew right away that a supporting character in *The Necromancer's Bones* was a ghost? That wasn't as important as how he died. And my best friend could tell which prince was hiring the assassins in *Too Many Princes*? Well, she didn't guess that the evil prince had been replaced by a doppelganger.

In both cases, having someone see the man behind the curtain pushed me to try harder on my plot. I added additional surprises and brought more depth to the characters, all to out-wit my first readers. Ultimately, I wrote a better book.

So as you work out your plot, remember there are readers out there who live for the thrill of guessing your surprises. Your job is to be sure there's more to the story.

Deby Fredericks has three fantasy novels published by Dragon Moon Press: *Too Many Princes*, *The Magister's Mask*, and its sequel, *The Necromancer's Bones*. www.debyfredericks.com

Surprising Yourself

by Susan Oleksiw

My writing advice is really a way of thinking about characters and plotting. When I begin a mystery novel I usually have a sense of how it will end and the character most likely to be the murderer. But then I stop and look at the entire cast of characters and imagine that each one could be the murderer, each one could turn out to have done something I don't yet know about.

I try to imagine the story from the many different perspectives of alternate murderers. This keeps me a little sharper, and opens up the story as I write. Nothing is set, and everything important can change. After this imaginative exercise, I no longer write as though I know the ending, and I no longer write worrying that I might give something away.

Susan Oleksiw is the author of the Mellingham series featuring Chief of Police Joe Silva, and the Anita Ray series, set in India. Her most recent book is *Under the Eye of Kali: An Anita Ray Mystery*, set in a resort in tropical South India. www.susanoleksiw.com

About the Authors

Chris Eboch writes in a variety of genres.

The Eyes of Pharaoh, set in Egypt in 1177 BC, brings an ancient world to life. When Reya hints that Egypt is in danger from foreign nomads, Seshta and Horus don't take him seriously. How could anyone challenge Egypt? Then Reya disappears. To save their friend, Seshta and Horus spy on merchants, soldiers, and royalty, and start to suspect even The Eyes of Pharaoh, the powerful head of the secret police. Will Seshta and Horus escape the traps set for them, rescue Reya, and stop the plot against Egypt in time? For ages nine and up. Available as paperback or e-book. Read the first chapter at www.chriseboch.com.

In *The Well of Sacrifice*, a Mayan girl in ninth-century Guatemala rebels against the High Priest who sacrifices anyone challenging his power. *Kirkus Reviews* called *The Well of Sacrifice*, "[An] engrossing first novel....Eboch crafts an exciting narrative with a richly textured depiction of ancient Mayan society.... The novel shines not only for a faithful recreation of an unfamiliar, ancient world, but also for the introduction of a brave, likable and determined heroine." Available as hardcover or e-book.

The Haunted series for ages 8-12 follows a brother and sister who travel with their parents' ghost hunter TV show. They try to help the ghosts, while keeping their activities secret from meddling grownups. In *The Ghost on the Stairs*, an 1880s ghost bride haunts a Colorado hotel, waiting for her missing husband to return. *The Riverboat Phantom* features a steamboat pilot still trying to prevent a long-ago disaster. In *The Knight in the Shadows*, a Renaissance French squire protects a sword on display at a New York City museum. During *The Ghost Miner's Treasure*, Jon and Tania help a dead man find his lost gold mine — but they're not the only ones looking for it. Available as paperback or e-book. Read excerpts at www.chriseboch.com.

Jesse Owens: Young Record Breaker and *Milton Hershey: Young Chocolatier* are inspirational biographies in Simon & Schuster's Childhood of Famous Americans series, written under the name M.M. Eboch.

Ms. Eboch also writes novels for adults under the name Kris Bock. *Rattled* brings romantic suspense to the dramatic and deadly New Mexico desert. Erin isn't used to adventures — except those in books. But when she uncovers a clue to one of the greatest lost treasures ever, she and her best friend Camie head for the New Mexico desert to search for a secret cave. They're not the only ones interested in the treasure, however, and they'll face more dangers than Erin ever imagined, from wild animals, wilder humans, and the wilderness itself. Fortunately Erin and Camie have help, in the form of one sexy helicopter pilot and an unusual orange cat. Available as paperback or e-book. Read the first three chapters at www.krisbock.com.

Guest Authors

Susanne Alleyn is the author of the Aristide Ravel French Revolution mystery series (*The Cavalier of the Apocalypse*, *Palace of Justice*, *Game of Patience*, and *A Treasury of Regrets*), and of *A Far Better Rest*, a re-imagining of *A Tale of Two Cities*. She is the granddaughter of children's author Lillie V. Albrecht, who penned the classic *Deborah Remembers* (1959) and four other historical children's books, all soon to reappear as e-books. www.susannealleyn.com

Vijaya Bodach is a scientist-turned-children's writer who has published over 60 magazine pieces and over 30 science books for young readers. www.vijayabodach.com

Jan Christensen is an author of over 50 published short stories and a novel, *Sara's Search*, in which amateur sleuth Sara learns secrets, meets quirky characters and dashes between metropolitan NJ and NYC to solve her father's murder. www.janchristensen.com

Douglas J. Eboch wrote the original script for the movie *Sweet Home Alabama*. He teaches at Art Center College of Design and lectures internationally. He shares screenwriting techniques on his Let's Schmooze blog. http://letsschmooze.blogspot.com/

Janet Fox writes fiction and non-fiction for children of all ages including the award-winning *Get Organized Without Losing It* and the young adult novel *Faithful* (Speak/Penguin, 2010), an Amelia Bloomer List pick. Her most recent work for young adults, the historical novel *Forgiven* (June 2011; Speak/Penguin), is a 2011 Junior Library Guild selection. She lives with her husband in Bozeman, Montana. www.janetsfox.com

Dorothy Francis is an award-winning author who writes short stories and novels, including the Key West mystery series. www.dorothyfrancis.com

Deby Fredericks has three fantasy novels published by Dragon Moon Press: *Too Many Princes*, *The Magister's Mask*, and its sequel, *The Necromancer's Bones*. www.debyfredericks.com

Janice Hardy offers more tips about writing on her blog, "The Other Side of the Story" (http://blog.janicehardy.com/). She's also the author of the teen fantasy trilogy The Healing Wars, where she tapped into her own dark side to create a world where healing was dangerous, and those with the best intentions often made the worst choices. Her books include *The Shifter*, *Blue Fire*, and the upcoming *Darkfall* from Balzer+Bray/Harper Collins. www.janicehardy.com

Sophie Masson has published more than 50 novels internationally since 1990, mainly for children and young adults. A bilingual French and English speaker, raised mostly in Australia, she has a master's degree in French and English literature. Her most recent novel to be published in the USA, *The Madman of Venice* (Random House), was written for middle school children, grades ~6-10 and her recent historical novel, *The Hunt for Ned Kelly* (Scholastic Australia) won the prestigious Patricia Wrightson Prize for Children's Literature in the 2011 NSW Premier's Literary Awards. www.sophiemasson.org

Jenny Milchman is a suspense writer from New Jersey. She is founder of the series Writing Matters, which draws authors and publishing professionals from both coasts to standing-room-only events at a local bookstore. In 2010 she created Take Your Child to a Bookstore Day, a holiday that went viral, enlisting booksellers in 30 states, two Canadian provinces, and England. Jenny is the author of the short story "The Very Old Man," an Amazon bestseller in mystery anthologies. Another short story will be published in 2012 in a book called *Adirondack Mysteries II*. Her novel, a literary thriller titled *Cover of Snow*, is forthcoming from Ballantine. www.jennymilchman.com

Mike Nettleton is co-author of *The Big Grabowski*, *Sometimes a Great Commotion* (sequel), *The Hard Karma Shuffle*, *The Crushed Velvet Miasma* (sequel), and *The Hermit of Humbug Mountain*. www.deadlyduomysteries.com/

Susan Oleksiw is the author of the Mellingham series featuring Chief of Police Joe Silva, and the Anita Ray series, set in India. Her most recent book is *Under the Eye of Kali: An Anita Ray Mystery*, set in a resort in tropical South India. www.susanoleksiw.com

Mary Reed co-authors the Lord Chamberlain historical mysteries and other tales of detection with her husband Eric Mayer. *Nine For The Devil*, the ninth novel in the Lord Chamberlain series, relates their protagonist's investigation into the death of Empress Theodora and will be published in March 2012 by Poisoned Pen Press. http://home.earthlink.net/~maywrite/

Suzanne Morgan Williams is the author of the middle grade novel *Bull Rider*, published by Margaret K. McElderry (Simon and Schuster). *Bull Rider* is a Junior Library Guild selection, Western Heritage Award Winner, and has been included on several state award lists. Besides working on fiction, Suzanne is author of several nonfiction books for children and young adults. Her newest nonfiction book is *China's Daughters*, from Pacific View Press. Suzanne is a frequent speaker at schools, libraries, writers' conferences, and teacher and librarian events. www.suzannemorganwilliams.com

Lois Winston is an award-winning author who writes the Anastasia Pollack Crafting Mysteries featuring magazine crafts editor and reluctant amateur sleuth Anastasia Pollack. *Assault With a Deadly Glue Gun*, the first book in the series, was a January 2011 release and received starred reviews from both Publishers Weekly and Booklist. *Kirkus Reviews* dubbed it, "North Jersey's more mature answer to Stephanie Plum." Lois is also an award-winning crafts and needlework designer and an agent with the Ashley Grayson Literary Agency. www.loiswinston.com

CPSIA information can be obtained at www.ICGtesting.com
Printed in the USA
LVOW011456110413

328761LV00020B/1041/P

9 781463 739300